THE ENTREPRENEUR'S GUIDE TO

Michigan Medical ***Marijuana Laws***

PATRICK T. BARONE, ESQ.

The Entreprenuer's Guide to Michigan Medical Marijana Laws /
Author. —1st ed.

ISBN: 978-0692968345 (Patrick T. Barone)
ISBN-10: 0692968342

Printed in the United States of America.

TABLE OF CONTENTS

Introduction

Many social and societal changes in the United States have occurred in the last several decades, and these changes have led to a more liberal view of marijuana. In turn, there has been a liberalization of state law as it relates to marijuana, and citizens in a majority of states have voted to approve either the recreational and/or medical use of marijuana.

In 2008, the citizens in Michigan joined this majority of states when a majority of voters agreed to allow the medical use of marijuana. This vote led to the creation of the 2008 law discussed in this book. Based on this law, people with a qualifying illness in Michigan could obtain a state sanctioned license that would allow them to legally produce, sell, and consume medical marijuana. This law also did several other important things. First, it created a structure where people with certain medical conditions could obtain a prescription for medical marijuana. Next, it provided a structure where a person with a valid prescription could obtain a permit or license that would allow them to purchase, possess, and consume medical marijuana. Finally, it provided an inchoate structure that allowed patients and caregivers to grow marijuana for medical use.

Because these laws were confusing, unclear, and caused many innocent people to be criminally prosecuted for laws they did not intentionally break, in 2016 a new series of laws were passed that accomplished three things; (1) added clarity to the patient/caregiver paradigm, (2) expanded and clarified when medical marijuana could be commercially produced and sold, and (3) provided for the tracking, from "seed to sale" of all commercially-produced medical marijuana in the state of Michigan.

These new laws have created if not encouraged a significant potential business opportunity for Michigan's citizens and entrepreneurs. Whether you have worked in the medical marijuana industry in the past, or your entrepreneurial instincts sense opportunity, these new laws have intrigue that may prompt you to seek a license. Many, with dollar signs in their eyes, have called the new laws a potential multi-billion dollar "gold rush!"

However, these laws are not for the uninitiated or inexperienced. Statutory, administrative, municipal, and common/case law can be difficult to understand and interpret. Add to this the further complications of the interplay between state and federal law, the need to keep meticulous records, to be well funded and insured and to have excellent bookkeeping, and one can see that a cavalier attitude toward a medical marijuana business won't work.

Furthermore, piecing together licensing information from many different resources can be tedious. In addition to this complication, successfully running a medical marijuana business requires a fair amount of business acumen. You will need some understanding of tax law, finance law, business law, intellectual property law, and conflicts of laws. For this reason, we've created this book. A chapter has been dedicated to each of these topics and this will allow you to have at least a general understanding of these topics. Reading these chapters will at least help you to know which experts you will need to assist you with your business endeavor, and know also what questions to ask and how you will need their help.

The conflicts of law chapter addresses the interplay between state and federal law. This is an important topic because marijuana continues to be listed as a "schedule one" drug on both the state and federal drug schedules. This means there is always the very real risk that the federal government, meaning FBI, district attorneys, and federal courts, could all work to extinguish any medical marijuana business interests in Michigan. Even if they don't move to close your business directly, the federal government could use civil forfeiture laws to seize property and assets. To further complicate the legal landscape, running afoul of the existing Michigan medical marijuana law might mean finding yourself charged with a serious state felony.

For these reasons, more than almost any other business, the only way to mitigate your personal and financial risks, and to accomplish fantastic returns on your capital, is to find and work closely with a Michigan medical marijuana legal expert. You will also need to find and use knowledgeable accountants, bank or loan officers, insurance professionals, and security experts. Some of Michigan's best professionals have written chapters in this book, and are available to assist you with your business needs.

Armed with the right cadre of experts, the business expertise, and the appropriate risk tolerance, medical marijuana can be an exciting, rewarding, and profitable business.

About This Book

This book provides a comprehensive step-by-step guide to Michigan's medical marijuana laws, including the following topics:

- The evolution of Michigan's medical marijuana laws.
- Summary of recent changes to Michigan's medical marijuana laws.
- Description of Michigan's five medical marijuana business licenses.
- Advice on how to start a successful medical marijuana business.
- Information to help you decide which of the five licenses is right for you.

- Advice on how to create and protect your business' intellectual property.
- Advice on how to safeguard your business and your employees.
- Advice on how to insure and finance your medical marijuana business.

If you are looking for one place to get all the information that you need to start a successful medical marijuana business in Michigan, you've come to the right place! However, this book is not a substitute for legal representation. When embarking on a new business venture, it is a good idea to retain an experienced attorney. Not only will this ensure that you properly qualify and properly apply for licensing, but it will also ensure that you remain in compliance throughout all your business practices. Please use this guide as a starting point for your research, then if you think a medical marijuana business might be right for you, retain legal counsel to join with you as you begin your journey!

A Note On Wording

We have made a few spelling choices throughout this book for consistency purposes. For example, there are two possible ways to spell the word "marijuana." There is the common and traditional spelling with a "j", but the word referring to the same thing/plant can also be spelled "marihuana."

Please note that all three of the medical marijuana related acts in Michigan use the word/spelling "marihuana." For example, the Medical Marihuana Facilities Licensing Act uses the "h" spelling, as does the Marihuana Tracking Act. For consistency and readability, except when referring to the acts themselves, we have attempted to always use the traditional spelling of "marijuana" with a "j."

On the other hand, as you review the Michigan laws themselves, either in the Appendices of this book, online, or elsewhere, you will see the spelling, "marihuana." Despite the different spelling, both terms refer to the same laws and acts.

"Cannabis" is another word that refers to marijuana. It may be used interchangeably with "marijuana" in this book and in other sources that you come across as well.

CHAPTER ONE

History of Medical Marijuana Laws in Michigan

Until very recently, the sale and use of marijuana was prohibited throughout the United States. But slowly, one after the next, a majority of states have adopted at least partial decriminalization and/or legalization of marijuana. States such as California and Colorado were some of the first to adopt policies allowing for medicinal or recreational use of marijuana. Since then, many states, including Michigan, have followed suit. In this chapter, I will discuss important events in Michigan that have impacted medical marijuana laws, and the relevant laws that have been passed. But first, let's examine the difference between decriminalization and legalization of substances such as marijuana.

Many states first decriminalize something, such as the use of medical marijuana, before they legalize it. Decriminalization means that it is still illegal to use or sell marijuana, but the penalties are less severe than if the substance was not decriminalized. Most people face relatively small penalties for possession and sale. For example, instead of jail time, those charged with marijuana related crimes might face a fine. In addition, having small amounts of marijuana, for example as medication, will likely be overlooked by the police. This is much the way it's been in Ann Arbor for many years.

Legalization, on the other hand, means that using or selling marijuana is no longer a crime. You cannot get punished for it at all, because it is no longer illegal to use or sell the substance. However, keep in mind that legalization also means regulation. You cannot simply grow or sell as much marijuana as you want. There are regulations set by the government that you need to follow to use the substance legally. This leads to the necessity of marijuana licensing and of course, taxation.

Legalization Timeline in Michigan

The process of legalizing something generally happens slowly over a long period of time. The remaining chapter will focus on important events in the past 10 years that have led to Michigan's current stance on terms of marijuana use and production.

2008

The legalization of marijuana in Michigan began in 2008, with the legalization of medical marijuana. In November of that year, a ballot proposal was created for Michigan voters. The proposal drafters wanted to give physicians the ability to approve the use of marijuana for a few serious medical conditions, such as AIDS and cancer. The proposal also asked that patients be allowed to grow marijuana for themselves, and for caregivers to have the ability to grow marijuana for their patients. The proposal passed, and the legalization of medical marijuana came into being in Michigan.

The proposal was turned into the Michigan Medical Marihuana Act (Hereafter "MMMA")[1], which became a law in December of 2008. The MMMA allowed both qualified patients and qualified primary caregivers to do a few different things. First, it allowed both parties to apply for an identification card and a spot on the state registry. Having an identification card protects patients and caregivers from prosecution of certain marijuana related crimes.

In addition, licensed patients and primary caregivers can grow and possess certain amounts of marijuana under the MMMA. A licensed patient can grow up to 12 plants for their own use, and a licensed medical marijuana caregiver can grow up to 12 plants for up to five patients. A person who is both a patient and a licensed medical marijuana caregiver can grow a total of 72 plants. In addition, a licensed patient can possess up to 2.5 ounces of usable marijuana.

Those licensed to grow and use marijuana under the MMMA are protected from criminal prosecution for growing and using medical marijuana. This protection is achieved using registry identification cards for those who qualify.

2009

Due to the MMMA, at the beginning of 2009, the state of Michigan received a lot of applications for registry and an identification card. The MMMA was approved in April 2009, and within two months the Department of Community Health approved 1,902 applications for medical marijuana registry. Since then, hundreds of thousands of applications have been received and approved by this department. Of course, not every application is granted, but there is still a considerable number of people in Michigan who have been approved by the state for the legal use of medical marijuana.

However, just because medical marijuana was approved at the state level does not mean that it was also decriminalized at the federal level. In 2009, the federal government made it clear that marijuana is still an illegal and dangerous substance. It is therefore still subject to criminal prosecution. However, through the Ogden Memo[2], the federal government implied that those who were in clear compliance with Michigan's state laws concerning marijuana would not be prosecuted for use or possession of medical marijuana. What constitutes "clear compliance" with the MMMA is not expressed, although the memo does give examples such as an illness for which marijuana is part of a treatment plan that complies with state laws.

In addition, the Ogden Memo outlined a few instances where clear and unambiguous compliance is not present. For example, this includes when marijuana is sold to minors, if the unlawful use or possession of firearms is present, or if a person has ties to criminal activity. Other examples include the illegal possession or sale of marijuana or other controlled substances, or if the marketing or financial practices of a person are not consistent with state laws.

The Ogden Memo applies to any state that has passed medical marijuana legalization laws, not just Michigan. Instead of addressing each state and situation separately, the Attorney General addressed each state in this blanket memo.

The MMMA did not address medical marijuana dispensaries, and many people took this as an opportunity to open such dispensaries where medical marijuana could be bought and sold. But these dispensaries were not protected under the MMMA, and therefore subject to prosecution. In fact, in the next few years, many of these dispensaries were shut down and prosecuted by the law. This would begin in Livonia, which passed a law prohibiting the use of enterprises in ways that will break local, federal, or state laws. Many other towns and counties in Michigan followed suit and created laws that prevented the legal use of medical marijuana dispensaries and medical marijuana in general in certain parts of the state. Still, the MMMA and other laws did not make it clear whether medical marijuana dispensaries should be allowed in Michigan or if counties had the right to ban them. This is an issue that would be settled in the next few years.

2010

In early 2010, Birmingham and Bloomfield Hills also enacted bans on medical marijuana dispensaries and medical marijuana use in their towns. These bans prompted backlash, led by the American Civil Liberties Union (ACLU)[3]. The ACLU sued cities that enacted medical marijuana bans, claiming that cities do not have the power to veto statewide laws. Despite the lawsuit, cities such as Wyoming continued to ban medical marijuana, prompting the state to take action.

Because of these bans and the backlash to them, the state of Michigan tried to rectify the ambiguity in the MMMA regarding important factors such as medical marijuana dispensaries. The Michigan Court of Appeals drafted their own opinion expressing the inconsistencies between the MMMA and the Public Health Code. These inconsistencies resulted in significant confusion and the Michigan Court of Appeals wanted to clarify the law. These issues would lead to a clearer stance on the use of marijuana and medical marijuana in Michigan.

2011

The United States Department of Justice expressed in the Cole Memo[4] that anyone in violation of the Controlled Substances Act was subject to criminal prosecution, regardless of state law. This stance was reinforced throughout 2011. First, this opinion was upheld when a federal judge ruled against a medical marijuana patient in *Casias v. Wal-Mart*[5]. In this case, a medical marijuana patient with a Department of Community Health issued registry card was terminated from his job at Wal-Mart after testing positive for marijuana. The judge ruled in favor of Wal-Mart, claiming that the MMMA did not regulate private employment. This ruling clearly indicates that even those with registry cards and those who follow Michigan's laws regarding medical marijuana can still face prosecution for marijuana related policies.

Furthermore, throughout 2011 the Court of Appeals ruled against medical marijuana dispensaries. For example, in *State v. McQueen*[6], the government ruled to shut down the Compassionate Apothecary, LLC on multiple grounds. Law enforcement used this ruling to crack down on various medical marijuana dispensaries throughout the state.

The state claimed that despite state laws, growing, distributing, or selling medical marijuana was still in violation of federal law under the Controlled Substances Act[7]. Michigan made it clear that those who participate in the business of medical marijuana are subject to federal prosecution.

In 2011, the Department of Justice also expressed in a medical marijuana legislative proposal that they do not focus their resources on prosecuting those who use medical marijuana to treat an illness in compliance with the Ogden Memorandum. However, the Department of Justice does reserve the right to prosecute such people as they see fit, even if an individual follows state laws.

2012

Despite the backlash to medical marijuana in various 2011 rulings, the court did protect medical marijuana users when it came to Michigan's zero tolerance driving policy related to drugs and alcohol. In the 2012 case of *People v. Koon*[8], the court found that the zero-tolerance policy does not apply to medical marijuana drivers. This means that for the state to convict a medical marijuana driver for DUI, they must prove that ability to drive was considerably impacted by the use of marijuana.

Case rulings in 2012 also saw a doctor's diagnosis as a viable defense to a marijuana charge. In addition, medical marijuana was approved for patients under the age of 18. At the time, there were 44 medical marijuana patients registered with the state who were under the age of 18.

In 2012, the court also ruled that the city of Wyoming needed to stop their ban on medical marijuana. The court claimed that Wyoming's law was unenforceable and void because it conflicted with the MMMA. The state recognized that the MMMA was still confusing in some situations and was difficult to interpret. In an attempt to clarify the MMMA, they signed several amendments to the MMMA into law in December of 2012.

Despite the amendments, later that same month Michigan's Supreme Court ruled that collective growth operations between caregivers and patients were not covered by the MMMA.

2013

Even though measures were taken to make medical marijuana more accessible in Michigan, the federal courts still ruled that marijuana is a dangerous substance. Efforts to change marijuana's classification as a "schedule 1" controlled substance did not affect its classification. What's more, "schedule 1" controlled substances are not viewed as having acceptable medical use. So, the federal courts still fought to prosecute marijuana related crimes.

In 2013, the *State v. McQueen* case was appealed. In the appeal, the Michigan Supreme Court continued to rule against medical marijuana dispensaries. They denied the appeal on the grounds that:

- Dispensaries are subject to prosecution from the state's public nuisance claim.
- The MMMA does not apply to dispensaries of medical marijuana.
- Affirmative defenses do not apply.

Another 2013 ruling by the Michigan appeals court determined that registered medical marijuana patients can exchange small amounts of marijuana. The court claimed that this was an action protected under the MMMA.

2016

Issues with dispensaries and collective growth operations continued in 2016. In *People v. Bylsma*[9], the court found that:

- Possession under MMMA means that a person has dominion over the substance.
- The defendant in the case controlled 88 marijuana plants, 24 more than were allowed under the MMMA.

A series of bills were drafted and in late 2016, passed into law. The hope was that this three-bill package would add clarity to the existing patient/caregiver paradigm, and also, provide a structure within which the commercial manufacture and sale of medical marijuana could take place. These bills are House Bill 4209, House Bill 4827, and House Bill 4210. The corresponding "Michigan Compiled

Laws" (MCL) are the Michigan Medical Marihuana Act (MCL secs. 333.26421 - 333.26430), the Medical Marihuana Facilities Licensing Act, (MCL secs. 333.27101 - 333.27801), and the Marihuana Tracking Act (MCL secs. 333.27901 - 333.27904). The first of these Acts amends and clarifies the patient/caregiver paradigm, the second outlines regulation and licensing information for the proper growth and sale of medical marijuana, and the third Act tracks the production and sale of medical marijuana throughout the state of Michigan. Each of these Acts is discussed in greater detail throughout this book.

This Chapter Written By: Patrick T. Barone, J.D. / Barone Defense Firm

CHAPTER TWO

Overview of Michigan's Medical Marijuana Laws

In the previous chapter, I discussed a basic timeline for marijuana related laws and events occurring in Michigan. In this chapter, I want to discuss a few of Michigan's medical marijuana related laws in more detail. Here, I will discuss MMMA information in more detail as well as the LARA medical marijuana program.

Michigan Medical Marihuana Act (MMMA)

Passed in 2008, the MMMA establishes many different provisions to assist those hoping to qualify for legal medical marijuana use. The original version of the MMMA protected qualifying primary caregivers and patients from various marijuana related crimes. Specifically, sections 4[1] and 8[2] of the Act set forth a variety of things that qualifying patients would be protected from under this Act, and provides certain defenses in the event of prosecution. Patients that have a registry identification card should not be arrested, prosecuted, or penalized for the use of medical marijuana. This includes getting penalized by a disciplinary board or for a civil issue. But, this is only the case if a patient uses marijuana in accordance with the MMMA. For example, the patient should not possess an amount of marijuana that exceeds the limit set by the MMMA. Patients also can't grow more plants than the MMMA allows. To prevent prosecution, the patient must present to the police a valid form of identification (such as a driver's license, state ID, or passport), as well as their registry identification card.

Under section 4(b), primary caregivers that are registered with the state are also exempt from prosecution. They will not be prosecuted for a qualified patient that is also registered with the state. Like patients, caregivers must provide a valid form of identification and their registry identification card to avoid prosecution. Violation of the MMMA can result in arrest or prosecution.

The MMMA also establishes what qualifies a patient to obtain a medical marijuana card. This Act lists the following medical conditions that make a person eligible for medical marijuana use in Michigan:

- Alzheimer's Disease
- Seizures
- HIV or AIDS
- Cancer
- Nausea
- Glaucoma
- Amyotrophic Lateral Sclerosis
- Chronic pain
- Post-Traumatic Stress Disorder
- Cachexia or wasting syndrome
- Hepatitis C
- Severe muscle spasms
- Nail patella

If you have one of these health issues, you could qualify for legal use of medical marijuana in Michigan. Obtaining a patient card under the MMMA will allow you to legally do many things. First, you can possess up to 2.5 ounces of usable marijuana. In addition, you can cultivate marijuana plants at home. You can grow up to 12 marijuana plants so long as you keep them in a secure, locked facility. If you are growing the plants outdoors, they cannot be visible from outside of your property. Also, you need to grow the plants within an enclosed structure. As a patient, you also need to register with the Department of Community Health to legally do these things.

If you are a caregiver of patients who have qualified for the use of medical marijuana and obtained the appropriate patient ID card, then you can also grow marijuana plants under the MMMA. To do so legally however, you must adhere to the following regulations. First, you must be at least 21 years of age. Also, you must never have been convicted of several different types of crimes. For example, you cannot currently face or have faced in your life a felony related to illegal drugs. You must never have been convicted of a felony related to violence. Also, you must never have been convicted of a felony of any kind in the past 10 years. Finally, you may only assist up to five medical marijuana patients (each patient can only have one caregiver).

Additionally, caregivers cannot possess marijuana in amounts or forms that violate the MMMA. The MMMA states that qualified primary caregivers can possess up to 2.5 ounces of combined usable marijuana equivalents and usable marijuana per patient. One issue that has been litigated in Michigan relates to the definition of "usable." In this unpublished case[3], 68 plants were found all in various states of dryness. The trial court ruled that "usable marijuana" "doesn't necessarily have to be dry and ready to smoke" and, thus, the 92.8 ounces of seized marijuana, not even considering the amount seized from the traffic stop, was more than the 15 total ounces that the defendant was permitted to possess under ¶ 4. In reviewing the trial court transcript, the Michigan Court of Appeals noted that with respect to the seized plant material from the building, the officer consistently testified that the marijuana was "green", "wet", "drying", or in the "drying states." The officer testified that, from his understanding, "usable marijuana could be also completely wet marijuana." The Court of Appeals found that "wet marijuana may, indeed, be 'usable' in some circumstances, it is not 'usable' for purposes of the MMMA. To be usable under the MMMA, the marijuana must be dried."

Additionally, when trying to determine usable marijuana equivalents, there are a few things that are the equivalent of one ounce of usable marijuana. This includes 16 ounces in solid form of a marijuana infused product, seven grams in gas form of a marijuana infused product, and 36 ounces in fluid form of a marijuana infused product[4].

Marijuana and marijuana paraphernalia related to this Act or used with medical marijuana by a qualified patient is not subject to seizure. In addition, caregivers can grow up to 12 marijuana plants per qualified patient, so long as the plants are kept in a secure, locked, and enclosed facility.

Each caregiver can have up to five patients, meaning they can grow a total of 60 plants. If they are also a patient, then this increases the number to 72 plants. This is the maximum number of plants a registered caregiver can ever grow without first obtaining a commercial medical marijuana growers license. However, a person cannot be both a registered caregiver and a holder of a medical marijuana grower's license. This preclusion prevents a grower/caregiver with a Class A license (allowing 500 plants)[5] from growing 572 plants. The details of all of this are discussed further in later chapters. Bear in mind that dominion and control may be enough to increase the number of plants each caregiver possesses. In a case finding that there may only be, "one caregiver per crop," the Michigan Supreme Court found that, "under the MMMA, possession of marijuana occurs when a person exercises dominion and control over it." Furthermore, that in a situation where 88 plants were found in a shared warehouse unit over which the defendant had "dominion and control" he possessed more than the 24 plants he was allowed[6].

Whether you are a patient, a caregiver, or a commercial license holder, you may wonder what exactly is a "plant." The only definition in the law indicates that "marijuana plant" means any plant of the species Cannabis Sativa L. This definition does not answer, for example, whether a cutting is a plant. This very issue was litigated in Michigan, and the Court of Appeals found[7], on an issue of first impression, that clone plants, which where portions of mature plants used to start new plants, were marijuana plants under the Michigan Medical Marihuana Act (MMMA)[8].

Of course, if a qualified patient or primary caregiver violates the MMMA, they are subject to arrest or prosecution. For example, if a registered patient or caregiver sells marijuana to a person who does not have a valid identification card, they face a possible felony conviction. They could be given a prison sentence of up to two years and could face a fine of up to $2,000[9]. These penalties are in addition to any other penalties that a person might receive for the distribution of marijuana.

The MMMA outlines a few penalties that caregivers and patients cannot face if they remain in accordance with the Act. For example, patients and caregivers can't be denied visitation or custody of a minor due to their medical marijuana cultivation, possession, or use (if applicable). Unless their behavior endangers the child, they are protected from losing rights concerning children.

Registered primary caregivers can also get compensated for costs related to the assistance of registered patients in using medical marijuana. Compensation in this case does not constitute sale of a controlled substance. However, the MMMA does not intend caregivers to be motivated by profit, and so caregivers may only charge a reasonable amount for costs associated in providing the marijuana. Growers motivated by profit should consider applying for and obtaining a commercial license.

In addition to protection for registered primary caregivers and patients, there is some protection for doctors under the MMMA. For doctors who do full, thorough examinations of patients and determine that they would benefit from the use of medical marijuana, the MMMA protects them from certain actions being taken against them. A doctor who does this and who provides a written certification stating this information cannot be arrested, prosecuted, or penalized. They also cannot have disciplinary action taken against them by the board of medicine in Michigan or the board of osteopathic medicine and surgery in Michigan.

LARA Medical Marihuana Program

Michigan's Department of Licensing and Regulatory Affairs (LARA) has established a medical marijuana program. Its purpose is to assist in the job creation and business growth that medical marijuana allows, while keeping Michigan citizens safe. LARA oversees the Michigan Medical Marihuana Program. You can visit the LARA website for important forms and information, including:

- The caregiver change form[10]
- Patient change form[11]
- MMMP minor application packet[12]
- MMMP application packet[13]
- Release for disclosure of information form[14]
- 2016 medical marijuana grant application
- 2017 medical marijuana grant application

For more information on these forms, read on.

Caregiver Change Form

To apply for caregiver change, you need to fill out the application, mail this application and any applicable documents to the Michigan Medical Marihuana Program, and pay the fee. On the form, you should specify a name change, address change, removing a patient, or requesting a replacement caregiver card. For these changes, you need to fill out and sign the change form, provide a valid form of photo identification, and pay a $10 fee.

Patient Change Form

For the patient change form, you need to do the same things as for the caregiver change form. In addition to these things, you need to specify a name change, address change, change of plant possession, removal of caregiver, request of replacement card, the addition of a caregiver, or the change of a caregiver.

MMMP Application

If you are over the age of 18 and you want to apply to the Michigan Medical Marihuana Program, mail the fee, a completed application, and the relevant documents to the Michigan Medical Marihuana Program. Make sure that you fill out an application for a registry identification card. Then, pay the fee ($60 for a patient, $25 for a caregiver). Also, make sure that you provide a copy of valid photo identification and the physician certificate form that has been signed by a doctor.

MMMP Minor Application

If you are under the age of 18, you can still apply to the MMMP, but separate provisions will apply. You need to fill out the minor application for a registry identification card. You also need to pay the $85 application fee and provide proof of your Michigan residency. Also provide proof of legal guardianship or parentage, and two physician certification forms that have been filled out and signed.

Release for Disclosure of Information Form

To apply for release for disclosure of information, fill out the form and get your signature notarized. Also provide a copy of your driver's license or your identification card. Then, you need to mail everything to the Michigan Medical Marihuana Program.

What is and is Not Legal Under the MMMA

It is important to keep in mind that just because medical marijuana has been made legal in the state of Michigan, this does not mean that anyone can grow and sell marijuana without repercussions. New acts and laws make certain activity related to medical marijuana legal, but they also create a framework for marijuana regulation. If a person violates these regulations, they are subject to prosecution.

If a business or a person unlawfully grows or sells marijuana, they will also be prosecuted. Remember that "unlawfully" in this context means violating either the letter or the spirit of the MMMA. This can happen innocently by simply failing to follow the dos and don'ts contained in the letter of the law. Be mindful also that the prosecution on your case might pursue both civil and criminal actions under the Controlled Substance Act[15] (CSA). So, if you do not follow proper marijuana regulations, you could face arrest and prosecution just as if you were a street level drug dealer. For example, you could get arrested for illegal manufacturing, distribution, possession, or delivery (sale) of a controlled substance (in this case, marijuana). The reverse is also true, and in one interesting Michigan case the Court of Appeals found that the uncompensated transfer of marijuana between patients constituted the medical use of marijuana as permitted by the MMMA[16]. However, you should know that simple possession of marijuana is a one-year misdemeanor under state law. (Of course, this is in reference to possession by a non-medical marijuana patient).

If this same crime is charged as under a city ordinance, the penalty will depend upon the jurisdiction. The penalties become much more severe when unlawful delivery is alleged. In this regard, depending on the amount "delivered," the delivery or manufacture of marijuana is often charged as a four-year felony. This charge would encompass scenarios where less than five kilograms of marijuana or 20 plants of marijuana are involved. As the amounts go up, so do the penalties. Thus, the alleged delivery or manufacture of more than five kilograms but less than 45 kilograms of marijuana is a seven-year felony, while the delivery or manufacture of 45 kilograms or more of marijuana can be charged as a 15-year felony.

You might be wondering how "delivery" would be proven in a court of law. Such evidence of intent to deliver is often based on direct evidence. This term is defined by the Michigan Standard Jury Instructions as follows: "direct evidence is evidence about what we actually see or hear. For example, if you look outside and see rain falling, that is direct evidence that it is raining[17]." Some examples of direct evidence might include the testimony of an undercover police officer who bought marijuana from you and observations made by a police officer of a "hand to hand" marijuana transaction.

The element of delivery in a criminal charge can also be proved by circumstantial evidence. This term is defined by the Michigan Standard Jury Instructions as follows: "circumstantial evidence is evidence that normally or reasonably leads to other facts. So, for example, if you see a person come in from outside wearing a raincoat covered with small drops of water that would be circumstantial evidence that it is raining[18]." Some examples of circumstantial evidence might include evidence of the possession of packing materials, such as those often used for the packaging of marijuana, the way the marijuana is packaged, the quantity of marijuana found (more than would be expected for personal use), the presence of a scale, large amounts of case, and particularly in denominations that support sales; and the lack of drug use paraphernalia.

In drug delivery cases, prosecutors also often use officers who are court qualified to testify as "experts" regarding this sort of circumstantial evidence. Such experts will offer their opinions as to why the circumstantial evidence found is consistent with the element of (shows the intent for) delivery. As relates to circumstantial evidence, the judge will tell the jury, "you may consider circumstantial evidence. Circumstantial evidence by itself, or a combination of circumstantial evidence and direct evidence, can be used to prove the elements of a crime. In other words, you should consider all the evidence that you believe.[19]"

You could also face an arrest for knowingly opening, leasing, renting, or maintaining a property that will be used to grow, distribute, or store illegal drugs. Manufacturing or distributing controlled substances within 1,000 feet of public housing facilities and within 100 feet of youth centers is another crime you might face. Also, you could get charged with using a communication facility to violate the CSA at the felony level. Then there is the conspiring to commit a crime against the CSA charge. Finally, you could face a charge for money laundering related to controlled substances.

It is important if you want to work with marijuana that you do so legally, and it may be necessary for you to hire an attorney to assist you in this endeavor. So long as you obtain the proper license and follow the regulations set forth by the government, then you should be able to do so without any adverse legal consequences. You can learn more about these licenses and regulations in the coming chapters. But before we get to that, it's important also for you to know that just because you are following state law, this does not necessarily mean you are protected from arrest or prosecution for violating a federal law. To understand why this is true, it is helpful to understand the interplay between state and federal marijuana laws, and these are discussed in the next chapter.

This Chapter Written By: Patrick T. Barone, J.D. / Barone Defense Firm

CHAPTER THREE

Conflicts of Laws

The Interplay Between Federal and State Regulation of Marijuana

As of January 2017, a total of 28 states have legalized medical marijuana. Seven states and the District of Columbia have approved the recreational use of marijuana. However, the federal government still categorizes marijuana as a "schedule 1" narcotic. What is the impact of federal law in those states where either recreational or medical use of marijuana has been approved by the state?

The Supremacy Clause

Article IV, Section 2 of the US Constitution is known as the Supremacy Clause because it provides that the, "Constitution and Laws of the United States shall be the supreme law of the land." This doctrine was first enunciated by Chief Justice John Marshall in *McCoullock v. Maryland*[1]. Justice Marshall declared that, "the government of the union, though limited in its power, is supreme within its sphere of action."

When a conflict arises between state action which is apparently incompatible with federal law, there are two issues that must be resolved. The first issue concerns whether the congressional action falls within the scope of federal authority. The authority of Congress to regulate drug trafficking within the United States has been well established for more than a century. The second issue centers around whether Congress intended to preempt state law. The test for determining whether Congress intended to preempt state law in the absence of a clearly stated intention to do so, has been outlined in *Pennsylvania v. Nebraska*[2]. In that case, the court suggested that the focus should be on whether the federal scheme is, "so pervasive as to make the inference that Congress left no room for the state to supplement it."

The analysis centers around the question that the federal interest is, "so dominant that the federal system must be assumed to preclude the enforcement of state laws on the same subject." Also, the second question concerns the possibility that enforcement of state law, "presents a danger of conflict with the administration of the federal program." It seems obvious that the decision of the states to permit the sale of marijuana for recreational use or even for a more limited purpose such as medical marijuana, is clearly in conflict with the federal enforcement scheme.

Clearly, the approval of the use, possession, cultivation, and distribution of marijuana even for the limited purpose of medical treatment, has caused a significant shift in the law. Until very recently, both sovereigns prohibited the use of marijuana. There was no conflict between the state and federal law and hence no issue that touched upon the Supremacy Clause.

Most likely, any federal court called upon to resolve the conflict between state law and federal law will be constrained to rule that the federal law is the supreme law of the land. Since the New Deal, courts have consistently expanded the power of the federal government at the expense of the state's ability to conduct its own affairs. Permitting the use, possession, distribution, and cultivation of marijuana, even for a limited purpose would, "present a danger of conflict with a federal program" if a state were to be allowed to legalize activities specifically prohibited by congressional action.

Dual Sovereignty

In *Heath v. Alabama*[3], the Supreme Court explained that the doctrine, "is founded on the common-law conception as an offense against the sovereignty of the government." Thus, the courts have held that even double jeopardy is not a bar to prosecution when the same act violates the peace and dignity of two sovereigns by the same act. In a state where the use of marijuana for medical or recreational purpose has been approved by the state government, there is no legal bar to the federal government enforcing its laws to prosecute an individual for a violation of federal law even though such conduct is permissible under state law. For example, in Michigan numerous courts have imposed upon defendants, who are released on bond or placed on probation, a prohibition against the use of marijuana even for those who have a medical marijuana card. The rationale for such a decision is that although the use of medical marijuana is legal under Michigan law, it constitutes a violation of federal law and hence constitutes a violation of law prohibited under standard bond conditions.

The change in Michigan law has created a conflict between state and federal law. Several states have authorized the use of marijuana for medical purposes. An additional group of states have legalized the recreational use of marijuana. However, it is abundantly clear that federal law still prohibits the use, cultivation, sale, possession, and distribution of marijuana. The question of what, if any action, the federal government anticipates taking against individuals who reside in states that have approved the medical or recreational use of marijuana is at present unclear. At the outset, the federal government will take a different position on the use of medical marijuana as opposed to recreational marijuana.

The Federal Government's Position on Medical Marijuana

A state law compliant medical marijuana business owner faces the prospect of arrest and subsequent prosecution by federal authorities. Moreover, such business owners are subject to both civil and criminal prosecution which could result in fines and forfeiture of property and other assets. In a criminal case, there is also the possibility of a substantial custodial sentence.

On August 29, 2013, US Deputy Attorney General James Cole issued a memorandum which described the approach US Attorneys in the 93 districts across the country were to take concerning the law in states that could be considered marijuana friendly. It is essential to understand that this memorandum does not have the effect of law and can be revoked at any time. It does not confer on anyone the right to avoid prosecution for a violation of federal law. The Obama Administration adopted a policy of slow playing or ignoring the enforcement of federal laws it deemed inappropriate. These actions did not and cannot create an expectation that a new administration will continue the same or similar policies.

As of this date, the Cole memorandum is still in effect and it does offer some guidance as to what federal policy may look like in the future. The memorandum identified eight priorities which were to be considered in evaluating whether the US Attorney should consider prosecution.

1. Does the state program insure that there will be no distribution to minors? A failure to effectively prohibit such sale would likely result to enforce federal law.
2. Does the statutory scheme insure that the proceeds generated by the marijuana business will not be transferred to criminal enterprises, groups, or cartels?
3. Does the state law prohibit the transportation of marijuana from a state where it is legal into a state where it is illegal?

4. Does the state regulatory system insure that the medical marijuana business will not be used as a cover for illegal activity including trafficking in other illegal drugs?
5. Is the use of firearms and violence in the sale and cultivation of marijuana prohibited by the state law?
6. Does the state law take steps to prevent drugged driving as well as addressing other adverse consequences associated with the use of marijuana?
7. Does the statutory scheme prohibit the cultivation of marijuana on public land?
8. Does the statutory scheme prohibit the use, possession, sale, and distribution of marijuana on federal land?

The Cole memorandum places great emphasis on the need for the state regulatory system to address these concerns. The federal government's reaction to state action will be predicated upon the, "expectation that state and local governments have enacted laws authorizing marijuana will implement strong and effective regulatory and enforcement systems that will address the effect that these state laws to public safety, public health, and other law enforcement interests." As noted earlier, the Cole memorandum is not in any way binding upon the present administration. Indeed, Attorney General Sessions has suggested that he may approach the matter in a very different manner, declaring on February 28, 2017 that, "states can pass the laws they choose. I would just say it remains a violation of federal law to distribute marijuana through any place in the United States, whether a state legalizes it or not."

There have been efforts in Congress to address the medical marijuana issue. The *Rohrabacker-Farr* or CJS amendment first passed in 2014 does nothing to address the problems posed by the US criminal code, which still classifies marijuana as a dangerous drug with no medical use. Rather, it is a budget amendment that prohibits the Department of Justice from using funds to prevent states from implementing medical marijuana. Since it is only a budget amendment, it needs to be reaffirmed every year.

Another development that those involved in the medical marijuana business should be aware of is the use of civil RICO by private litigants to seek damages from those involved in the medical marijuana business. This civil/criminal statute carries with it very significant financial penalties when used to initiate a civil action. Like anti-trust litigation, there is a provision for terrible damages in the event of an adverse decision. Could a group of physicians or pharmacists file a RICO lawsuit alleging damages based upon loss of revenue because individuals have chosen to use marijuana instead of FDA approved treatment? Would the damages be three times the amount of marijuana sold?

Another issue to be considered is that of firearms. Federal law makes the possession of a firearm in connection with a drug trafficking offense a felony. 18 USC 924(c) makes it a crime to possess a firearm during the commission of a drug offense. If you are engaged in a medical marijuana business, it is possible to consider any firearm you may possess as being part of your business. A firearm at your place of business, on your person, or in your vehicle could give rise to a charge of possession during a drug offense. Indeed, under certain circumstances even a firearm in your home could pose a problem. The best advice is to avoid firearms entirely. If you are a hunter or recreational shooter, storing the guns away from your house or business is an option to be considered.

This Chapter Written By: Keith Corbett, J.D. / Barone Defense Firm

CHAPTER FOUR

Significant Amendments
to the Michigan Medical Marihuana Act

As previously noted in Chapter 1, the original Michigan Medical Marihuana Act (MMMA), which was Initiated Law 1 of 2008[1], created many legal problems for those who were trying to safely and legally use medical marijuana. Eight years later, in 2016, an attempt was made by Michigan's legislators to clarify and perfect the 2008 initiated law. This package of statutory changes became the legislatively passed 2016 House Bill 4210. This Bill, which was primarily a package of amendments to existing medical marijuana statutes, was signed into law in December 2016. These amendments addressed and modified the pre-existing laws found in MCL § 333.26421 to MCL § 333.26430. The purpose of this chapter is to explain and discuss these amendments/changes, and how they might impact you either as a patient, caregiver, or commercial medical marijuana entrepreneur.

Overview of Amendments to the Michigan Medical Marihuana Act

House Bill 4210, which became the amended Michigan Medical Marihuana Act, mostly focuses on marijuana infused products, what qualifying patients and registered primary caregivers can and can't do, and more. The phrase "marijuana infused product" means a topical formulation, tincture, beverage, edible substance, or similar product containing any usable marijuana that is intended for human consumption in a manner other than smoke inhalation[2].

In terms of marijuana infused products, the amendments prevent qualified patients and registered primary caregivers from being penalized if they manufacture marijuana infused products. The amended MMMA also prohibits patients from transferring marijuana or marijuana infused products to other people and prohibits caregivers from transferring marijuana infused products to anyone except for their registered patients. In addition, the amended MMMA prohibits caregivers and patients from possessing or transporting marijuana infused products in motor vehicles, unless under special circumstances[3].

There are many other specifics related to these amendments to existing law that I will discuss in this chapter. Read on for more information.

Relevant Definitions[4]

The amended MMMA uses certain language that you might not be entirely familiar with. It is important to understand the legal definitions of certain terms moving forward. For example, the amended MMMA oftentimes refers to the term "marijuana infused product," which was defined above. Another oftentimes confusing term is "usable marijuana." This type of marijuana currently refers to dried flowers, leaves, extract from the plant, or plant resin of the marijuana plant. It also includes any preparation or mixture of these flowers and leaves[5]. However, usable marijuana does not refer to the stalks, seeds, or roots of the marijuana plant. Furthermore, "marijuana plant" gets defined as any plant in the species *Cannabis Sativa L* [6].

For registered patients and primary caregivers, it is also important to understand what the term "medical use of marijuana" means. This term refers specifically to the cultivation, possession, acquisition, use, manufacture, internal possession, transfer, delivery, or transportation of marijuana or marijuana paraphernalia to treat a registered patient. This term refers to both marijuana and marijuana infused products.

In previous chapters, I have discussed many of the illnesses that qualify a person to legally use medical marijuana. House Bill 4210 introduced the term "debilitating medical condition" to assist in specifying what medical conditions can be treated with marijuana. Debilitating medical conditions include specific diseases, such as cancer, HIV, glaucoma, Alzheimer's disease, acquired immune deficiency system, nail patella, hepatitis C, Crohn's disease, and amyotrophic lateral sclerosis. In addition, this term refers to a debilitating or chronic disease that causes one or more of the following symptoms: chronic and severe pain, epilepsy, severe and consistent muscle spasms, seizures, multiple sclerosis symptoms, and severe nausea. LARA is also permitted to approve some other medical condition for marijuana treatment. This is fortunate because it seems medical marijuana is being used effectively to treat an ever-increasing list of medical conditions. As such, this statutory list is already proving woefully inadequate. However, it's not easy to convince LARA to add new medical conditions, and attempting to do so will likely require legal assistance.

Marijuana Infused Products[7]

House Bill 4210 was amended to the prior Michigan Medical Marihuana Act to clarify and set forth new procedures for manufacturing, transferring, and possessing marijuana infused products. Under the amended MMMA, qualifying patients who register with the Department of Licensing and Regulatory Affairs have the right to:

1. Medical use of marijuana (so long as it is within the limits outlined in the Act).
2. Manufacturing marijuana infused products for their own use.

Similarly, a registered primary caregiver has the right to possess and manufacture medical marijuana for their qualifying patients.

Still, patients and caregivers are not allowed to do certain things when it comes to medical marijuana. Patients can't sell marijuana or marijuana products to other people, and caregivers can't sell marijuana or marijuana products to non-qualifying patients. Patients and caregivers also cannot possess or transfer marijuana infused products in a motor vehicle unless a patient carries the marijuana infused product in a sealed and labeled container in the trunk or in some other way so it is not readily accessible to the driver. The label should state the name of the manufacturer, date of manufacture, weight in ounces, name of buyer, and date of receipt.

Also, a caregiver cannot carry marijuana infused products in a motor vehicle unless they follow the instructions listed above. The label of the package should state the name and address of the manufacturer, name and address of the destination, date of manufacture, weight in ounces, date/time of departure, estimated date/time of arrival, and date of receipt.

If a registered primary caregiver has a spouse, parent, or child who is a registered patient, they can transport or possess a marijuana infused product in their vehicle in the same way as listed above. There is a $250 civil fine for patients and caregivers who do not follow these transportation rules.

Amount of Marijuana for Legal Possession[8]

Both qualifying patients and registered primary caregivers are legally allowed to possess marijuana and marijuana infused products. But, there is a limit to how much they can possess. Under the amended MMMA, both parties can only possess up to 2.5 ounces of usable marijuana. The amended MMMA states that a person cannot possess more than 2.5 ounces of usable marijuana and usable marijuana equivalents. This further breaks down to 16 ounces of a marijuana infused product in a solid form, seven grams of marijuana infused product in a gaseous form, or 36 fluid ounces of marijuana infused product in liquid form. In addition, incidental amounts of marijuana stalks, seeds, and roots are not included in the marijuana amount. These incidental elements are allowed under the amended MMMA.

Protection for Medical Marijuana Use

As I've explained in previous chapters, registered patients and primary caregivers are protected by the amended MMMA. The amended Act outlines specific provisions for protecting patients, primary caregivers, and physicians.

If patients are following the amount for legal possession of marijuana rules, and comply with the other regulations outlined in this amended MMMA, they will be protected from state and local civil and criminal prosecution. In addition, they will not have privileges taken away or face a sanction by a disciplinary board. The only way for patients to be prosecuted for marijuana related offenses is if they do not follow the rules of the bills and they do not present their identification card or a government issued photo identification card when prompted. The same rules and protection applies to registered primary caregivers.

If a primary caregiver or a patient has a registry identification card and an amount of marijuana in their possession that does not exceed the limit, it is presumed that they are engaged in the use of medical marijuana under this amended MMMA. This presumption protects the patient or caregiver from arrest. But, evidence can prove that the patient or caregiver's conduct was not in compliance with the amended MMMA. If this is the case, the patient or caregiver could face civil or criminal charges.

Most of the time, patients and caregivers are not allowed to possess or transport marijuana or marijuana infused products. However, there are some situations where this is possible. Now that the Medical Marihuana Facilities Licensing Act has been enacted, registered patients and caregivers have other rights. They cannot be arrested, prosecuted, or punished for purchasing or transferring an authorized amount of marijuana from a licensed provisioning center. They also cannot be prosecuted for selling or transferring marijuana seedlings or seeds to a licensed grower. Finally, they cannot be prosecuted for transferring marijuana to and from a licensed safety compliance facility.

Finally, the amended MMMA outlines protection for physicians. While physicians cannot provide marijuana, they can prescribe it as part of a patient's treatment. As long as a written certification for marijuana is the result of a full evaluation of the patient's medical history, the physician cannot face certain penalties. For example, the physician cannot face civil or criminal penalties. In addition, they can't face sanctions from the Michigan board of medicine or the Michigan board of osteopathic medicine and surgery. They also can't face sanctions from any other board or business. If it is determined that the physician failed to evaluate the patient's medical condition properly, or if they violated the standard of care in any way, they can be subject to sanctions from a professional licensing board.

Scope of Protection

While the amended MMMA allows patients and caregivers to do many things, there are certain things that are not permitted under the law. These restrictions are outlined in the amended MMMA. For example, even with a registry identification card, a person cannot do something under the influence of marijuana if that task would be negligent. For example, this might include operating heavy machinery or going to work under the influence of marijuana. In addition, patients and caregivers cannot possess marijuana on a school bus, on school grounds, or in a correctional facility. They also cannot smoke marijuana in a public location or on any form of public transportation.

You also can't operate a motor vehicle, aircraft, motorboat, off road recreational vehicle, or snowmobile while under the influence of marijuana. You should not use marijuana unless you have a debilitating medical condition. Finally, you can't separate marijuana plant resin by butane extraction in a public place, a motor vehicle, a residential building, or in a way that does not exercise care for the safety of others.

A Note on Operating Under the Influence of Marijuana

Having a medical marijuana card that allows you to consume medical marijuana does not always protect you from prosecution for the crime of operating while intoxicated[9]. This is because the principle crime in Michigan is called OWI, meaning operating while intoxicated. This crime can be proved by showing the driver was intoxicated by either alcohol or drugs.

If the crime is OWI-drugs, then there are two theories available to the prosecutor, either OUID or operating under the influence of drugs or OWPD, meaning operating with the presence of drugs. OWPD is for zero-tolerance drugs, including marijuana. What this means is the prosecutor need not show that the marijuana had any impact on your driving, only that you used marijuana before you drove. A medical marijuana card holding patient is protected only from this zero-tolerance theory. If you have used medical marijuana and are in operation of a motor vehicle, vessel (boat), aircraft, snowmobile, etc., and the officer believes that you are operating it while "under the influence" of marijuana, then you can be prosecuted under the OUID theory.

The applicable jury instruction defines "under the influence" this way:

> "Under the influence of a marijuana" means that because of using or consuming marijuana the defendant's ability to operate a motor vehicle in a normal manner was substantially lessened. To be under the influence, a person does not have to be falling down or hardly able to stand up. On the other hand, just because a person has smells of marijuana or used marijuana does not prove, by itself, that the person is under the influence of marijuana. The test is whether, because of using marijuana the defendant's mental or physical condition was significantly affected and the defendant was no longer able to operate a vehicle in a normal manner.[10]

Thus, if you have used medical marijuana, and the prosecutor can prove that the marijuana caused you to no longer be able to operate a motor vehicle in a normal way, then you can be found guilty of OWI.

As it relates to a driving under the influence of marijuana case, the "indicia of intoxication" analysis is significantly different from that applicable to a driving under the influence of alcohol case. In an alcohol case, an officer will most often indicate that he/she was able to detect the odor coming from the person, even when the odor is first detected coming from the car with multiple occupants. By contrast, in a marijuana case, the marijuana odor is almost always coming from the car. It is often difficult to isolate the odor as coming from a person. Thus, if there is more than one person in the car, then without an admission to smoking, it may be difficult for the officer to determine that the driver is the person responsible for the odor. Also, unlike alcohol, the odor of marijuana tends to linger long after it was last smoked. For these reasons and others like them, the odor of marijuana alone may be insufficient to establish probable cause for arrest.

In a case addressing this very issue[11] the defense, on behalf of his client Mr. Ford, brought a motion to dismiss for lack of probable cause to arrest. This motion required an evidentiary hearing, and several witnesses testified at the hearing. The first was the deputy dispatched to investigate a report of vehicles racing on an oval track on frozen Lake Winnebago. When he got close to Ford's car he could smell marijuana, and claimed that Ford acknowledged having smoked it within the past half-hour. On cross-examination, the deputy also acknowledged that he did not have probable cause to arrest for OWI based on Ford's performance on field sobriety tests.

A second deputy contradicted this testimony in part, in that he testified that Ford never admitted smoking marijuana, but instead said others in the car had been smoking. Also, that he never retrieved any marijuana from the car. The defendant testified that when the two deputies approached him in his vehicle they stated they could smell marijuana but he told them "somebody else" had been smoking in the vehicle prior to him getting in it; he never told them he himself had smoked marijuana. Also, that he passed field sobriety tests. Nevertheless, Ford was arrested, his blood was drawn, and he was charged with operating a motor vehicle with, "a detectable amount of a restricted controlled substance in his ... blood."

Following the hearing, the circuit court issued its decision, drawing parallels between this case and another case involving a defendant named Graske[12]. The circuit court indicated that, "in *Graske* they indicate [an odor of marijuana coming from the car] by itself without a link to more is insufficient evidence for the arrest for driving while under the influence of a controlled substance so I think the officer had every right to go through the process but I don't think there is probable cause in the end for the arrest, and so for that purpose I'm going to suppress the blood test that was because of the arrest."

The court of appeals indicated, somewhat contrary to the circuit court opinion, that, "an odor of burnt marijuana creates an inference that marijuana is not only physically present in the vehicle, but that some of it has been smoked recently."[13] However, since there was no evidence that Ford was alone in the vehicle, the court found that, "the County failed to meet its burden to establish the link between the odor of marijuana and Ford's personal consumption of the drug as the source of that odor" and thus affirmed the circuit court.

This Chapter Written By: Patrick T. Barone, J.D. / Barone Defense Firm

CHAPTER FIVE

Understanding Michigan's Medical Marihuana Facilities Licensing Act

The Medical Marihuana Facilities Licensing Act, as set forth in Michigan Compiled Laws, §§ 333.27101 - 333.27801, creates the regulatory framework for each of the five available licenses. The word "framework" is specifically chosen because these series of statutes do not comprise the entire regulatory landscape. This is because these statutes don't come fully into definition, use, or application without the corresponding administrative rules. These administrative rules will be drafted by the Michigan Department of Licensing and Regulatory Affairs (LARA).

If you are currently a patient or caregiver, then you are familiar with LARA. These administrative rules will include the actual license application, cost, number of licenses available, and so forth. Although this information is not yet available, by contacting a lawyer you can learn more about what this regulatory framework might look like. This chapter is devoted to House Bill 4209, also known as the Medical Marihuana Facilities Licensing Act.

Overview of Medical Marihuana Facilities Licensing Act

House Bill 4209 became the series of laws known as the Medical Marihuana Facilities Licensing Act, which is set forth in MCL § 333.27101 to MCL § 333.27801. This Act does many things. First, it provides licensing for those who commercially grow, process, transport, provide, and test marijuana (as mentioned in the previous chapter). It also establishes a licensing process with the Department of Licensing and Regulatory Affairs (LARA). The Act also creates the Medical Marihuana Licensing Board, which oversees licensing and the operation of medical marijuana facilities. In addition, the Medical Marihuana Facilities Licensing Act requires fees to both apply for and maintain a medical marijuana license. Fees to maintain the license will go into a Marijuana Regulatory Fund, which will be used for administering and enforcing this Act.

Also consider that it requires provisioning centers to pay a tax related to their retail gross income. This tax goes into the new Medical Marihuana Excise Fund. The money in this fund goes to places where marijuana facilities exist. Money from the fund also goes to State Police, the Michigan Commission on Law Enforcement Standards, and the State General Fund (until September 2017). After September 2017, the money will go instead to the First Responder Presumed Coverage Fund.

In addition, this Act authorizes the Marihuana Licensing Board to impose fines and license suspensions if someone violates the rules set in place. The Bill imposes restrictions on board members, agents, and employees to prevent conflict of interest. For those who are properly licensed and following the regulations, it exempts them from marijuana related prosecution. It also does this for those who are registered medical marijuana patients and caregivers. It also requires LARA to create emergency rules with the Board. The Act requires those who have licenses to use a third-party inventory tracking and control system. It also requires those who have licenses to prove to LARA that they have the financial ability to pay for liability of harm to marijuana users caused by adulterated marijuana. Finally, the Act creates the Marihuana Advisory Panel, which makes recommendations to the Marihuana Licensing Board.

Application Regulations Under the Medical Marihuana Facilities Licensing Act[1]

Many of the individual statutes contained within the Medical Marihuana Facilities Licensing Act, as set forth in Michigan Compiled Laws §§ 333.27101 - 333.27801, address license applications and eligibility. I discuss some application information and eligibility requirements in other subsequent chapters, but here I will also outline the regulations listed under MCL §§ 333.27101, *et. seq.*

Before you apply for a license, you should make sure that you are eligible for that license. You don't want to go through the time and money of filling out an application if your application will be immediately denied by the Board. Here are the disqualifications for those who apply for one of the new marijuana related licenses:

- You were convicted or released from conviction for a felony within the past five years.
- You were convicted of a controlled substance, dishonesty, theft, or fraud misdemeanor in the past five years.
- You have been convicted of a controlled substance related felony within the past 10 years.
- You submit a knowingly false application.
- You are a member of the Medical Marihuana Licensing Board.
- You can't maintain adequate casualty insurance or premises liability for the facility.
- You want to open a facility in a municipality that is not authorized for marijuana facilities yet.

- You hold elective office.
- You are a member or employee of a regulatory body of the government.
- You are employed by a governmental unit in Michigan.
- Until June 30, 2018, you will be ineligible if you have not been a Michigan resident for the past two years before applying.

There are other issues that are not immediate disqualifications, but that can have an impact on the Board's decision. For example, the Board will consider if you filed for bankruptcy in the past seven years. In addition, they consider the source and amount of your capital to run the facility and your history of noncompliance with regulatory requirements. Finally, they will take into consideration if you are a defendant in a litigation case involving your current business practices.

One of the first steps in obtaining your license is filling out the application under oath[2]. You must do this on an application provided by the Medical Marihuana Licensing Board. This application will ask for information such as your name, business address, and phone number. You also need to provide your Social Security number and your Federal Tax ID number (if applicable).

Then you need to provide the name of every person who has ownership interest in you and your application. This includes names and addresses of beneficiaries if the application is for a trust, names and addresses of shareholders, directors, and officers if the applicant is a corporation, names and addresses of partners if the applicant is a limited liability partnership or a partnership, and names and addresses of any managers if the applicant is a limited liability company.

You should also provide identification of businesses involved in businesses that grow, process, transport, test, or sell marijuana and information regarding if the applicant has been indicted, charged, arrested, convicted, or pled guilty to a criminal offense. This relates to controlled substance misdemeanors or any felony charge. Information regarding if the applicant has applied for or received a certificate or commercial license by a Michigan licensing authority or a licensing authority in some other jurisdiction must also be provided. You must state if such a license was ever denied, suspended, restricted, not renewed, or revoked.

You should also provide information regarding if the applicant faced a complaint or similar notice filed with a public body for delinquent payment or dispute of payment for a tax required under local, state, or federal law. Then, give a list of names and titles for officers and public officials, as well as their children, spouses, and parents, if they directly or indirectly have an interest in the applicant. This might include financial, beneficiary, or contractual interest.

You also need to give a description of the proposed marijuana facility as well as an estimate for actual/anticipated employees and receipts—whether gross or projected. Provide a paper copy of the ordinance that the municipality used to authorize the operation of the marijuana facilities within the municipality. Finally, provide your financial information, a copy of notice informing the municipality of the application, and any additional information that the Board requests.

Along with this application, an applicant must submit a passport quality photograph of themselves, a set of fingerprints for every person with ownership interest in the facility, a set of fingerprints for everyone who is a manager, director, or officer in the facility, and the application fee.

If you want to apply for a license, know that the Board can use the information on the application to conduct a background check on you. You need to provide consent for such a search. False or incomplete applications will not be accepted. If you have an interest in some other state operating license, your application will also be denied.

Once you get the license, you are not done. The license is awarded for a one-year period. After this, you need to apply for license renewal[3]. The Board will renew licenses if the licensee applies for renewal with a renewal form that is properly filled out.

They will also renew a license if the application is sent in on or before the date that the current license expires. Make sure that you pay the renewal fee and meet the renewal requirements, or your license won't be renewed.

If the Board does not receive the renewal application by the one-year expiration date, it can still be renewed within 60 days following the expiration date. In this case, the license could still be renewed if a renewal application in sent in, if it meets the requirements, and the late licensee holder submits a late fee.

The Medical Marihuana Licensing Board[4]

The Medical Marihuana Facilities Licensing Act, as set forth in Michigan Compiled Laws §§ 333.27101 - 333.27801 also outlines the Medical Marihuana Licensing Board (also known simply as, the Board). This Board will consist of five members and it will work within LARA. Members of this Board must be residents of Michigan. They also must be appointed by the Governor of Michigan. In addition, they must be from different political parties (no more than three members from the same party). They get appointed from three nominees by the State Majority Leader (for one member), and get appointed from three nominees from the Speaker of the House (for one member). In addition, one member of the Board will be appointed by the Governor as the Chairperson.

Members hold their position on the Board for a period of four years. This occurs with the one exception that those appointed for the first time carry out different terms. One member will serve for two years and two members will serve for three years. If a member expresses a sense of neglect for their duty, malfeasance, misfeasance, or nonfeasance, they can be removed from the Board. This also applies for some other just cause. Board members are also not allowed to hold any other public office that they get compensation for while they serve on the Board.

A person becomes ineligible to act as a Board member if they are not in good moral standing. In addition, an indictment, charge, or conviction for a misdemeanor for controlled substance, theft, dishonesty, or fraud, or any felony, will disqualify a person from becoming a Board member. Other issues that prevent someone from becoming a Board member are having a similar license in another state, or having a family member who has a licensing application pending before the Board.

To apply for a position on the Board, every potential applicant must file a financial disclosure statement with the Governor. They must provide a list of their liabilities, assets, business interests, property, and source of income. They also need to provide a financial disclosure statement for their spouse. Other important aspects of being a Board member deal with what happens after their position with the Board ends. For two years after their position on the Board ends, Board members cannot establish interest or be employed by a licensee, an applicant, or a marijuana facility. In addition, former Board members cannot represent anyone but the state before the Board for the two years after termination. The Governor has the right to remove any Board member if they neglect to do their job or for any other just cause.

The Medical Marihuana Licensing Board's job is to follow and implement the Medical Marihuana Facilities Act. Their tasks are related to regulating and enforcing the licensing and regulation system that is part of the Act. This relates to licensing and regulating licenses for marijuana growth, processing, transportation, and testing. There are many other duties, for example denying or granting applications for state operating licenses. This must happen in a reasonable amount of time from when the application was submitted. Those on this Board also need to make decisions for license applications in an order that seems reasonable. It is also their responsibility to implement and collect the license application fee, the tax on provisioning center, and the regulatory assessment.

In addition, they need to provide for the collections of fines and levy for violation of rules within the Act and oversee marijuana facilities through auditors, inspectors, and agents. The Board reviews and rules on complaints filed by licensees on investigations on their businesses that they believe are inappropriate. In addition, they hold two or more public meetings per year and review patterns of marijuana transfers by licensees. In addition, they must make recommendations to the legislature and Governor in an annual written report and oversee marijuana facilities to make sure that products meet health and safety standards.

They are also responsible for reviewing complaints by licensees, and they can make rulings on these complaints. If a licensee is subject to an investigation that they believe is unnecessary, the licensee can complain to the Board.

The Board must maintain their own records that are separate from other state board records. These records are public and they need to state all Board proceedings. They should conduct periodic audits of the licensed facilities.

The Medical Marihuana Licensing Board has the power to oversee operation of all marijuana facilities. They have the authority to investigate applicants, figure out if they are eligible for a license, and grant or deny licenses based on the rules of the Act. They also have the right to investigate any employee of a marijuana facility. The Board can audit, inspect, or examine relevant records that the licensee has. If the licensee does not cooperate with this investigation, the Board can still obtain these records. The Board also has the right to inspect any licensee holder or their property while they are at a marijuana facility. The Board requires that all relevant records stay at the marijuana facility.

Licensees should also submit to the Board a list of any stockholders that have 1% or more investment in the company. If an individual does not submit to the Act rules, they can be ejected from the marijuana facility.

Another important thing that the Board must do is investigate alleged violations of the Act. They also need to take appropriate measures if a provision of the Act was violated.

LARA and the Board have the right to set emergency rules[5] when necessary. These rules will be related to the administration, implementation, and enforcement of this Act. Some examples of appropriate rules include setting appropriate standards for marijuana facilities and their equipment. In addition, they can establish minimum insurance levels that licensees must meet. They can establish additional operating regulations for the different types of licenses. Also, they can establish restrictions and qualifications for people who are involved in the marijuana facilities.

They can establish testing procedures, standards, and requirements for marijuana that is sold through provisioning centers. In addition, they can provide for the collection and levy of fines if someone violates the Act. They can also require the use of the statewide monitoring system. For marijuana facilities, they can establish quality of control requirements, chain of custody requirements, waste product storage and disposal requirements, chemical storage requirements, marijuana storage requirements, labeling and packaging requirements, and transportation requirements. In addition, they have the right to establish advertising and marketing restrictions, maximum tetrahydrocannabinol levels in marijuana infused products, health standards, and restrictions for edible marijuana infused products.

Sanctions[6] and Hearings[7]

If a person applying for a license or a person who has a license fails to comply with the Medical Marihuana Facilities Licensing Act, the Board can deny, revoke, suspend, or restrict their license. This is also the case for licensee holders that do not meet the eligibility requirements anymore, or if that person does not comply with the Marihuana Tracking Act. Finally, this is the case if a licensee fails to cooperate and assist the Board in an inquiry, investigation, or Board hearing.

The Board can also impose sanctions on those who do not follow the Medical Marihuana Facilities Licensing Act. They can give a civil fine of as much as $5,000 against a person and up to $10,000 against a licensee for each of their violations of the Licensing Act or orders given out by the Board. Of course, the Board must comply with the Administrative Procedures Act if they are going to impose a fine or restrict, revoke, or deny a license.

In many cases, if the Board is going to suspend or revoke your license, you have the right to a hearing. But, if the Board determines that the safety and health of the employees or patrons of the facility are in jeopardy, the Board can suspend the license before a hearing is scheduled. If this happens, a hearing after the suspension takes place must be scheduled. This hearing will determine if the suspension should continue. The suspension will continue until the Board sees cause that the suspension should be lifted. Alternatively, the Board can revoke the license.

If a person's application is denied, they can request that a public investigative hearing take place. The applicant can then present testimony to show that they are suitable for the license. The Board will then review their decision, although this does not always mean that a license will be granted.

Anyone who is unhappy with a decision that the Board makes has the right to schedule a hearing with the Board. A person must send a written request for such a hearing within 21 days of receiving the Board's decision.

Marihuana Advisory Panel[8]

The Medical Marihuana Facilities Licensing Act introduces a Marihuana Advisory Panel, a part of LARA that will make recommendations to the Medical Marihuana Licensing Board. This panel may make suggestions concerning rules. In addition, if the Board asks for assistance with administering, implementing, and enforcing the Marihuana Tracking Act and the Licensing Act, the panel can do this.

This panel is made up of 17 members, including:

- The Director of State Police.

- The DHHS Director.
- The Attorney General.
- The LARA Director.
- The Director of the Department of Agriculture and Rural Development.
- A registered medical marijuana patient.
- A registered medical marijuana caregiver.
- A representative of medical marijuana growers (appointed by the Governor, along with the remaining people in this list).
- A representative of processors.
- Provisioning centers representative.
- Safety compliance facilities representative.
- Township representative.
- Sheriff's representative.
- Counties representative.
- Cities/villages representative.
- Local police representative.
- Secure transporters representative.
- Licensed physicians' representative.

All panel members must serve for at least three years, or until a replacement is appointed subsequently. Within one month of the panel members being appointed, the LARA Director must call a meeting. At this meeting, the panel will appoint a chairperson. After this initial meeting, the panel should meet twice a year (at least). In addition, this panel is subject to the Open Meetings Act.

Marihuana Facilities[9]

The Medical Marihuana Facilities Licensing Act states that marijuana facilities can only exist in municipalities under certain circumstances. The municipality must have an ordinance that authorizes marijuana facilities. Municipalities have the right to adopt ordinances that allow one or more types of marijuana facility within its boundaries. In addition, they can establish an ordinance to limit the number of marijuana facilities and types of marijuana facilities. The municipality also has the right to establish zoning regulations and other ordinances in its jurisdiction. However, it can't interfere or conflict with statutory regulations that pertain to licensing marijuana facilities. This solves the issues of certain areas in Michigan passing legislation to ban marijuana dispensaries and facilities.

After a municipality receives notice from an applicant that they have applied for a marijuana related license, the municipality must contact the Board with certain information. Within 90 days, they need to provide the Board with a copy of the ordinance that allows the marijuana facility. They also need to provide a copy of zoning regulations, if any apply to the proposed facility. They should also let the Board know if the applicant broke any zoning regulations or local ordinances related to the MMMA or the House Bill. If the municipality does not provide this information to the Board, the applicant will not be penalized for this. If there are enforcement or administrative costs related to the marijuana facility in a certain municipality, the municipality can charge the licensee up to $5,000 per year to defray these costs.

Inventory Control and Tracking System[10]

All people with licenses must use a third-party inventory control and tracking system. This system must be capable of interfacing with the statewide monitoring system. This allows licensees to obtain information that is already in the system or enter new information into it. In addition, the inventory control and tracking system must have the ability to do many things. It must track all marijuana products, plants, packages, waste, conversions, transfers, patient purchase totals, primary caregiver purchase totals, sales, and returns. It also must track batch and lot information through the whole chain of custody and track marijuana plant, batch, and product destruction.

Also consider that it must track the transportation of the product, track and report loss, diversion of product, or theft of marijuana, negative patient responses as well as dose efficacy issues, report sales, and refunds.

The Inventory Control and Tracking System also must electronically obtain and transmit information required under the MMMA, the Licensing Act, and the Marihuana Tracking Act. It must electronically obtain test results from safety compliance facilities through a secured application program.

Then, it must directly link test results to the applicable sample and batch, identify possibly altered test results, and provide access to information in the system that the licensee needs to carry out marijuana transactions. It must cross check that sales were made to registered patients or caregivers and that the product sold was properly tested.

The system must provide certain things to officials as well. It must provide state agencies, LARA, law enforcement agents, and licensees with information that they need.

The system also must secure confidentiality for the information that it contains. It must provide LARA with analytics about daily sales, plants being produced, plants being destroyed, and inventory adjustments. Finally, it must perform complete batch recall tracking.

If you have a marijuana related business, your system only needs to provide you with information that you need based on the type of license that you have.

Protection from Prosecution/Sanctions[11]

While the Medical Marihuana Licensing Board and other entities can impose certain sanctions on licensees, there are some things that they cannot do. Except in circumstances that are otherwise provided, a licensee and its agents are not subject to certain penalties. They are not subject to criminal or civil penalties related to marijuana at the state or local level. Please note that the Medical Marihuana Facilities Licensing Act does not protect licensed individuals who face federal charges. The federal government can still prosecute those who break federal laws related to controlled substances.

In addition, these parties are protected from inspection or search, unless it is one authorized by the Marihuana Licensing Act and seizure of real or personal property, including marijuana, based on a marijuana offense. Those with licenses also cannot face a sanction, denial of a privilege, or disciplinary action based on marijuana related offenses.

Licensed commercial entities are not subject to inconsistent provisions in acts such as the Nonprofit Corporation Act, the Business Corporation Act, the Uniform Partnership Act, the Michigan Limited Liability Company Act, and the Michigan Revised Uniform Limited Partnership Act.

Those who have licenses are not the only ones with protection from certain sanctions. A property owner or lessor will not face criminal penalties, prosecution, inspection, search or seizure, or other sanctions if they lease property to a license holder and are unaware of the licensee's violation of the Marihuana Licensing Act. These property owners or lessors cannot face state or local civil and criminal penalties, nor will they be subject to inspection and search. The only situation in which inspection will be authorized is if the municipality, the department, or law enforcement conducts a search under the Act.

So long as they purchase the quantity of marijuana within the legal limit from a provisioning center, registered patients and caregivers cannot be sanctioned for their purchase. In addition, a registered primary caregiver cannot be sanctioned for transporting 2.5 ounces or less of marijuana to a testing facility.

If a person has a state license, they can do things within the scope of this license. These tasks might include growing, purchasing, selling, receiving, transferring, transporting, possessing, processing, testing, extracting, infusing, or altering marijuana.

This Chapter Written By: Patrick T. Barone, J.D. / Barone Defense Firm

CHAPTER SIX

Should I Apply for a Commercial Medical Marijuana License?

Now that you have a general overview of the laws of Michigan, and how they interplay with federal law, it's time to take a closer look at whether the medical marijuana business is right for you. Once you've completed your due diligence relative to the exploration of this potential business opportunity, you may want to turn your attention to deciding if you should consider applying for a license. This chapter can help you decide if getting a medical marijuana license is right for you. I will discuss what licenses are available, and the important factors of each, such as what possessing a license allows you to do. I will also discuss some benefits of being a license holder, and some of the potential pitfalls as well.

Commercial medical marijuana was ushered into Michigan in late 2016 through the passing and signing of House Bills 4209, 4210, and 4287. These Bills eventually became three new Acts, and each Act is itself a series of individually numbered statutes or laws. These statutes are set forth in what are now the Michigan Medical Marihuana Act[1], the Medical Marihuana Facilities Licensing Act[2], and the Marihuana Tracking Act[3]. Collectively, these Acts allow the licensing of:

- Marijuana cultivation[4]
- Marijuana processing[5]
- Marijuana sales through provisioning centers, also known as dispensaries[6]
- Marijuana safety compliance and testing facilities[7]
- Marijuana transportation[8]

In addition to these state-granted licenses, medical marijuana entrepreneurs will also need to work with their local governments to procure the local licenses and permits required to establish a medical marijuana business. This is because a municipality in which you want to operate must pass an ordinance which authorizes the type of facility you wish to open. The municipality must receive notice from you that you have applied for any one of the five licenses. Like a liquor license, a municipality must also approve your request to have your license transferred, sold, or purchased.

What's Allowed Under the New Laws and Licensing?

Although House Bill 4209 did alter the Michigan Medical Marihuana Act, if you are a medical marijuana patient or caregiver, little has changed. However, for caregivers and other people who want to commercially grow and provide medical marijuana related products, the new licensing laws establish protection and regulations that did not exist previously. These laws and protections govern the proper growth, transportation, testing, and sale of medical marijuana. In the past, there was a great deal of uncertainty relative to these categories. Under the previous legal paradigm, if you possessed, transported, or sold medical marijuana, then it was relatively easy to run afoul of the state's criminal laws. People who engaged in such activities publicly, including for example the opening and running of a medical marijuana dispensary, were often unfairly subjected to an arrest and prosecution. Even if that didn't happen, it was likely they would lose their investment due to the shutting down of the facility. This was all happening under the "old" law because the MMMA was not clear about what was and was not allowed in terms of dispensing marijuana. The MMMA refers to and primarily addresses marijuana consumption by medical patients. It did very little to clarify how the marijuana can be distributed. In other words, it required but did not allow a variety of business relationships.

Even in the light of all this, in some areas of Michigan, the police wouldn't bother you if you wanted to grow or sell medical marijuana to appropriate patients. But, in other counties, the police would shut down these facilities, and you could face criminal charges. However, the Medical Marihuana Facilities Licensing Act[9] and the Marihuana Tracking Act now provide a framework for regulations for those who want to legally and commercially transport, cultivate, test, process, or sell medical marijuana. Although these activities were required by the MMMA, they were not specifically allowed. Contrary to the old paradigm, these new laws mean that so long as you follow the regulations set forth within these new laws, you should not be arrested for your marijuana business, nor should you risk losing your invested capital or property. Consider these key changes.

Clearer Regulation - the Creation of the Medical Marihuana Licensing Board

As in the past, the Department of Licensing and Regulatory Affairs (LARA) will regulate medical marijuana sales. In addition, a new Medical Marihuana Licensing Board[10] will play an important part in regulation of medical marijuana businesses. For example, this Board has the general responsibility for implementing this Act. They will also be responsible for reviewing business license applications. However, it is important to note that the Board will not be allowed to promulgate a rule establishing a limit on the number or type of marijuana facility licenses that may be granted[11].

On the other hand, they will have the authority to approve these applications and grant licenses. The Board will provide oversight of marijuana facilities through inspectors, agents, and auditors, and through the state police or attorney general. Using these agents, the Board will certify revenue, conduct investigations into the operation of marijuana facilities, and will be responsible for promoting the security and integrity of the operation of marijuana facilities. The Board will hold open meetings, and will assist the State's governor and legislature through their review of the patterns of marijuana transfers under this Act. This review of the tracking database will be used in and for the administration and enforcement of this Act.

Taxes and Other Fees[12]

Taxes and other fees will apply to medical marijuana businesses. These taxes and fees must comply with Michigan's sales tax. In addition, there will be a 3% tax at the register for patients using new provisioning centers. Businesses are also subject to additional fees. Businesses applying for a license must also pay fees as part of the application process. There are also investigation and processing fees not covered by the application fee.

Once licensed, licensees must also pay an assessment fee every year. This includes an annual, nonrefundable fee (of up to $5,000) to be set by, and paid to, your local municipality. These fees are used to offset administrative and enforcement costs associated with the operation of a marijuana facility in the municipality.

Finally, in evaluating medical marijuana as a business, you need to consider the fees associated with violating one of the statutes or laws in the running of your business. You will be protected from prosecution of marijuana related crimes, but only if you comply with the regulations outlined for your license. You face fines and other consequences if you violate the terms of your license.

Medical Marijuana Businesses

There are several types of marijuana related businesses mentioned in the new laws. These businesses include:

- **Marijuana growers:** These businesses will cultivate medical marijuana.
- **Marijuana processors:** These businesses will extract marijuana or infuse extractions of marijuana into various products.
- **Marijuana safety and compliance facilities:** These businesses will test marijuana and provide analytics.
- **Marijuana dispensaries:** these businesses will facilitate the commercial transfer of medical marijuana from growers/processors to lawful patients.
- **Secure marijuana transporters:** These businesses transport medical marijuana from one facility and/or location to another.

If you decide to get a medical marijuana license, you should determine which part of the process you want to partake in.

Marijuana Cultivation / Growers

Businesses that cultivate medical marijuana will be subject to limits under new regulations. These limits will be based on the class of license that you receive. If your business has a Class A license, you can grow up to 500 marijuana plants. If your business has a Class B license, you can grow up to 1,000 marijuana plants. Finally, if your business has a Class C license, you can grow up to 1,500 marijuana plants. These limitations might impact which class of license you secure because the more plants, the larger and more expensive the business. As many entrepreneurs already know, larger isn't always better, and larger certainly doesn't always mean more profitable.

Marijuana Processing

Unless smoked, before marijuana can be consumed by a patient, it must be prepared or "processed" for such consumption. Businesses that make marijuana "edibles" would want this kind of license. More broadly stated, those businesses with a processor's license can purchase marijuana from a grower, and then extract resin from it. They are also able to create marijuana-infused products.

Marijuana Testing, Compliance, and Safety Labs

To assure quality and safety, medical marijuana and medical marijuana products must get tested before they can be sold. Testing labs will be designed to test marijuana for CBD and THC levels before the product is ready for sale. They will also test for unsafe contaminants in the marijuana. All of this occurs at the testing labs, also known as safety compliance facilities.

Marijuana Transporters

Those who move medical marijuana and medical marijuana products between businesses must have their own license. This is a transportation license. These transporters do not have ownership of the marijuana. They also cannot arrange the contracts of other businesses.

Under the new laws, all employees and provisions regarding marijuana are protected in a legitimate medical marijuana business. For licensed facilities and for those who rent property from licensees, there are limitations on search and seizure by the police.

Marijuana Selling / Provisioning

According to the new laws, the commercial selling of marijuana will take place at "provisioning" centers. A provisioning center is any commercial property where marijuana is sold at retail. The operative word here is "commercial." A noncommercial location used by a caregiver to assist a patient connected to the caregiver is not a provisioning center. Provisioning centers will obtain their products directly from either a commercial grower or provisioner.

What Business Activities are Legally Protected?

Michigan's Medical Marihuana Licensed Facilities Act (MLFA)[13] provides legal protections for only certain business activities, so it's important to know what is and is not a protected activity. First, to have legal protection, meaning protection from certain kinds of civil or criminal prosecution, you must have first been granted a state operating license and be operating within the scope of the license. If both are true, then you and your agents are not subject to criminal penalties or criminal prosecution. You are also free from any search or inspection not otherwise provided by the MLFA. The government also may not seize your marijuana, or any real or personal property based on a marijuana-related offense. This means the state of Michigan may not pursue civil forfeiture of your marijuana, property or money. However, see Chapter 3 regarding the conflict of state and federal laws in this regard.

Finally, provided you have a state granted license and are operating within it, you are free from any disciplinary action or denial of a right or privilege, by a business or occupational or professional licensing board based on a marijuana-related offense. These protections apply also to those who own or lease real property to a business operating under the MFLA. You may give up this protection, however, if you have knowledge that the licensee violated MFLA.

As indicated, only certain business activities under the MFLA are protected. These include growing, purchasing, receiving, selling, transporting, or transferring marijuana from or to a licensee, registered qualifying patient, or a registered primary caregiver. Possessing or manufacturing marijuana paraphernalia for medical use is also a protected activity, as is processing and transporting marijuana. The MFLA also specifically indicates that properly licensed businesses acting within the scope of their licenses, may also test, transfer, infuse, extract, alter, or study marijuana.

Why Obtain a Medical Marijuana Business License?

Medical marijuana can help people with debilitating diseases like no other drug. As research continues to be done, more scientists are demonstrating its efficacy at treating a wide range of medical, emotional, and physical disorders. For many, medical marijuana is indeed a "miracle drug." In addition to helping others, a medical marijuana business can be fun, exciting, and profitable; and without a license you are breaking the law. Thus, the simple answer to "why obtain a license" is because you want to help people and because you desire to own and/or operate a business related to the growing, processing, provisioning, transporting and/or testing of medical marijuana. On the plus side, now that there are regulations to protect your business, and you stay in strict compliance with them, you won't have to worry about getting shut down or having your property or money seized by the state government.

If you are a caregiver interested in becoming part of a medical marijuana business, obtaining a commercial license can help you reach more patients. You won't be restricted to growing marijuana plants in the double digits. Instead, you can grow hundreds or thousands of plants, which means that you can help more patients than ever before.

If you think that beginning a medical marijuana business and getting a license are things that you are interested in, check out the next chapter for information about the different licenses.

This Chapter Written By: Patrick T. Barone, J.D. / Barone Defense Firm

CHAPTER SEVEN

Which Commercial Medical Marijuana License is Right for Me?

As discussed in the last chapter, there are many different types of licenses for which you might want to apply before taking part in a medical marijuana business in Michigan. The Medical Marihuana Facilities Licensing Act[1] establishes the five licenses available. These licenses include the growing license, processing license, provisioning license, secure transportation license, and safety compliance license.

In this chapter these licenses are discussed in greater detail. This discussion will help you determine which license might be best for you.

Growing License

As I stated in the previous chapter, the growing license allows a person or business to cultivate and process medical marijuana. If you are currently a caregiver, you might consider getting this type of license. However, as discussed elsewhere, you can't hold both a caregiver license and a grower's license. Nevertheless, having a grower's license will allow you to continue doing what you already do, yet on a larger scale. This license will allow you to legally assist more medical marijuana patients because you may grow on a much larger scale than you may as a caregiver.

The medical marijuana growing licenses in Michigan can be broken down into three categories - Class A licenses, Class B licenses, and Class C licenses. With a Class A license, you can grow up to 500 marijuana plants. With the Class B license, you can grow up to 1,000 plants. The Class C license is the license with the most freedom, as you can grow 1,500 plants with this.

A grower license allows you to sell marijuana seeds or plants only through a secure transporter. In addition, it allows you to sell marijuana to a provisioning center or a processor.

Eligibility and regulations for this license include:

- The applicant and investors have no interest in a safety compliance facility or a secure transporter. This means that you cannot also have these types of licenses if you have a grower's license.
- Until December 3rd, 2021, the applicant must have at least two years of experience working as a registered primary caregiver. Alternatively, they must have a person with this experience as an active employee in their business.
- You need to enter all current inventory and transactions into the statewide monitoring system.
- You can't operate in an area unless it has been zoned for agricultural and industrial uses. Alternatively, the area must be un-zoned and meet local requirements.

You must use a licensed transporter when buying or selling seeds or plants. Also, you may only sell your products to a licensed medical marijuana processor or provisioning center. Direct sales by growers to patients is strictly prohibited. *Violating this section of the Act may result in the revocation of your grower's license and/or criminal or civil prosecution*. To be eligible for a grower license, you (and all your investors) must not have an interest in a secure transporter or safety compliance facility.

You must also possess, or have as an active employee, an individual with a minimum of two years' experience as a registered primary caregiver. (This requirement currently ends December 31, 2021). However, you may not currently be a registered primary caregiver and may not employ an individual who is currently a registered primary caregiver. The purpose of this requirement is to limit your number of plants to only that allowed by the license class. You will not be able to add plants by adding caregivers. With limited exceptions, having a grower license does not authorize you to operate in an area not specifically zoned for industrial or agricultural uses. Finally, you must enter all transactions, current inventory, and other information into the statewide monitoring system as required by the Marihuana Tracking Act.

If you are interested in growing medical marijuana for sale on a large scale, this is the type of license that you should get.

Processing License

A processing license is like a growing license, but it applies to a place as opposed to a person. This means that the license applies to a commercial facility. This facility buys marijuana from a grower or a place that grows marijuana. A processing license can allow a company to buy marijuana and extract resin to create marijuana infused products. The facility can then package and transfer these products to a provisioning center.

This type of license only authorizes purchase of marijuana from a grower. The processing license also only allows sale to a provisioning center. Marijuana can also only be transported by a secure transporter. To have this type of license, you or your investors can't also have an interest in a safety compliance facility or a secure transporter. The regulations and eligibility for this license are the same as for the grower's license. In fact, these eligibility rules and regulations apply to all licenses.

Provisioning License

Provisioning licenses apply to provisioning centers. After marijuana is grown and processed, it goes to a provisioning center. This center acts as the retail seller, also known as the medical marijuana dispensary. The provisioning license allows the center to sell directly to medical marijuana patients or their caregivers.

A provisioning center license only allows you to obtain marijuana from a grower or a processor. You can only sell or transfer marijuana to a registered primary caregiver or a registered patient with this license. Again, transporting marijuana must happen through a secure transporter. You can also send marijuana and marijuana products to a safety compliance facility, but only through a secure transporter.

Before you can sell marijuana to a patient or a caregiver, you need to check with the statewide monitoring system to make sure that the patient or caregiver is registered and that the sale won't exceed the daily purchasing limit that the Medical Marihuana Licensing Board establishes.

The sale or consumption of alcohol or tobacco is also prohibited in a provisioning center. In addition, a doctor cannot conduct a medical exam or give out registration ID cards to patients on the premises.

Secure Transporter License

Transporting medical marijuana between these various licensed facilities also requires its own license. You need a state license if you intend on transporting marijuana from one place to another. But, keep in mind that this license does not allow you to deliver marijuana from a provisioning center to a caregiver or a patient.

This license will also allow you to store and transport both marijuana and money related to it between marijuana facilities. The marijuana must go to a facility - not an individual patient or a caregiver. Eligibility for this license requires that the applicant and their investors cannot have a vested interest in a person who has another type of license. They also can't be a registered caregiver or patient.

A safety compliance licensee also must:

- Have a chauffeur's license provided by the state of Michigan.
- Have at least two people traveling with the marijuana, and at least one person remaining with the marijuana always.
- Establish a route plan and enter this into the statewide monitoring system. If stopped by law enforcement, the driver must provide a copy of this route.
- Keep the marijuana in sealed containers that are not accessible during transfer.
- Make sure that the vehicle transporting marijuana does not have markings that indicate the transfer of marijuana.

Note that the transporter can be subject to inspection by the police at any time during the transfer.

Safety Compliance License

Safety compliance centers test marijuana for things like contaminants before it can be sold. In addition, marijuana will get tested for levels of tetrahydrocannabinol and cannabinoids. This information will go on the packaging for the marijuana.

Such a facility must be accredited by an entity that the Board has approved. This must happen within one year of the license being issued. Or, the facility must have provided drug testing services to the state in the past, or it must be a vendor that has good standing for this service. The Board can grant a variance of this requirement if necessary. Eligibility for this license requires that the applicant cannot have a vested interest in a person who has another license. A safety compliance facility also must do the following.

First, they must perform tests that certify that marijuana is free (to a reasonable degree) of chemical residue such as insecticides or fungicides. They also must use validated testing methods to test the levels of THC, THC acid, CBD, and CBD acid in the marijuana. In addition, they must determine if the marijuana complies with Board standards for mycotoxin and microbial content. Then they must perform tests to determine if the marijuana complies with good manufacturing practices. They also must enter inventory and transactions into the statewide monitoring system. They must secure lab space that is not accessible by the public. Finally, they must make sure that they employ at least one staff member with an advanced degree in a related field, such as laboratory or medical sciences.

Applications

If you want to get a marijuana license, you should make sure that you are eligible before you spend the time and money applying. You will be considered ineligible of applying for this license if:

- You have been convicted of a felony within the past 10 years.
- You have been convicted of a misdemeanor involving theft, dishonesty, or a controlled substance.
- You previously filed an application for a grower's license that you knew contained false information.
- You are a member of the Medical Marihuana Licensing Board.
- You are an elected official.
- You can't provide proper premises liability or casualty insurance.

Other factors that will be taken into consideration include:

- If you have applied for bankruptcy in the past seven years.
- If you have a history of tax issues.

- If you have ever skipped bail.
- If you have a prior history of business problems.
- If you have ever been charged with a crime.
- Your financial situation.
- Your moral character.

If you think you meet these eligibility requirements, then the first thing you must do is prepare your application for a license. In this regard, you will be an applicant. The law provides that an "applicant" is a person who applies for a state operating license. Also, the Act indicates that the term "person" can refer to an individual, corporation, limited liability company, partnership, limited partnership, limited liability partnership, limited liability limited partnership, trust, or other legal entity[2]. Because business entities may also apply for licenses, the Act also uses the term applicant to refer to an officer, director, or managerial employee of the applicant.

The state of Michigan is carefully evaluating all individuals who might have an interest in the medical marijuana business, so the Act also used the term applicant when referring to a person who holds any direct or indirect ownership interest in the applicant (if not an individual)[3].

Preparing your Application

Beginning December 20, 2017, a person (see above definitions) may apply to the board for state operating licenses in the categories of Class A, B, or C grower. The application shall be made under oath on a form provided by the Board and shall contain a large amount of information.

As you would expect, the application process begins with providing your name, business address, business telephone number, social security number, and, if applicable, federal tax identification number. If you are a corporation, then the application must disclose the names and addresses of all shareholders, officers, and directors. If you intend to form a partnership or limited liability partnership, then the application must include names and addresses of all partners.

You must also disclose if you have ever been indicted, charged with, arrested for, or convicted of, pled guilty or nolo contendere to, forfeited bail concerning any felony or controlled substance-related misdemeanor, not including traffic violations. You must also include the date, the name and location of the court, arresting agency, and prosecuting agency, the case caption, the docket number, the offense, the disposition, and the location and length of incarceration.

Information regarding any licenses you may hold in other states, or that have been revoked or denied or suspended in other states must also be included. You must also disclose any information relative to legal issues you've ever had paying your taxes or not paying your taxes. Also, the application will require you to include a description of the type of marijuana facility you envision; the anticipated or actual number of employees; and projected or actual gross receipts. This should all be included in your business plan, and can be copied from it to the application.

Finally, if the Medical Marihuana Licensing Board determines that the applicant is qualified to receive a license under this Act then you must pay both the nonrefundable application fee required under the regulatory assessment established by the Board for the first year of operation[4]. If you meet all the requirements, and are not excluded for any reason, then the Board shall issue you a license.

Background Checks for all Employees

You may not hire anyone to work for your business, in any capacity, if they have a controlled substance-related felony within the past 10 years. However, the Michigan state marijuana board may allow you to hire such an employee provided you notify them and they give you permission. To comply with this law, you must complete a background check, subject to the laws of Michigan.

Proof of Financial Responsibility

You will not be able to obtain a license without first providing proof of your "financial responsibility," which in this context is essentially proof of liability insurance. The Act specifically requires that you obtain insurance to reimburse someone for bodily injury suffered because of the manufacture, distribution, transportation, or sale of adulterated marijuana or adulterated marijuana-infused product. The insurance must be for at least one hundred thousand ($100,000.00) dollars. However, since obtaining insurance can be difficult considering marijuana remains a "schedule 1" drug, the proof of financial responsibility may be in the form of cash or unencumbered securities or a constant value bond. You are not allowed to cancel your insurance as required unless you give 30 days' notice to the department, and provide a reasonable and acceptable substitute.

For purposes of liability under this Act, the term "adulterated marijuana" means a product sold as marijuana that contains a chemical or biological matter other than marijuana that causes an "adverse reaction." The law does not define what is and is not an adverse reaction, so it is likely that this will be litigated in the future. In the meanwhile, be aware that appropriate compliance testing at a reputable licensed testing facility is a must because it will help protect you against false claims of adverse reactions. There is also an exception to what is covered as bodily injury and that relates injuries that may result in the normal course of the long-term use of marijuana or marijuana infused products. This includes any adverse effects from smoking marijuana, so long as the adverse effects are not a result of an adulteration of the product.

Compliance with Tracking Act

As a license holder in Michigan, you must comply with all aspects of the Act, and this includes compliance with the Marihuana Tracking Act (MTA). The MTA requires that growers use a seed-to-sale cloud based computer application approved by the state of Michigan. This Tracking Act requires use of a "statewide monitoring system" which is an internet-based, statewide database. This system will be established, implemented, and maintained by the state of Michigan under the Marihuana Tracking Act. The system must be available to licensees, law enforcement agencies, and authorized state departments and agencies on a 24-hour basis.

The tracking system will be used for (i) verifying registry identification cards, (ii) tracking marijuana transfer and transportation by licensees, including transferee, date, quantity, and price, (iii) verifying in commercially reasonable time that a transfer will not exceed the limit that the patient or caregiver is authorized to receive under Section 4 of the Michigan Medical Marihuana Act[5].

Financial Reporting Requirements

You won't be able to keep your commercial medical marijuana license for very long unless you can keep excellent records. The cloud based computer system will certainly help, but like any successful business, you must adopt systems and processes that will help you track all your income and expenses. Such detailed records are an absolute necessity because you are required by the Act to transmit to the Board and to the municipality, once per fiscal year, financial statements of your total operations. Not only must you keep good records, but these records must be reviewed by a certified public accountant. Compliance with this part of the Act is just one more business expense that you must be prepared to assimilate into your overall operating budget and business plan.

Violations of the Act

Your state granted commercial medical marijuana license does not give you a property right[6]. It is a "revocable privilege," meaning the state of Michigan can take your license from you. This means that if you violate the Act, or another applicable and relevant law, then your license can be revoked, suspended, or restricted. Your license is also exclusive to you as the licensee[7].

Certain activities will result in the revocation, suspension, or restriction of your license. For example, if you fail to comply with the Act or if you fail to properly utilize a tracking system, or if you fail to continue the eligibility requirements under this Act, then the state may take action against your license. Also, if you fail to provide information the Board requests to assist in any investigation, inquiry, or board hearing, the Board may deny, suspend, revoke, or restrict a license. The same is true relative to your employees.

If you are found to be in violation of the Act, then you may be fined up to five thousand ($5,000.00) dollars. Also, you may be fined based on an amount equal to your daily gross receipts or up to ten thousand ($10,000.00) dollars, whichever is greater. Such fines are applicable to each violation, so it is quite possible for fines to reach numbers high enough to devastate your business.

Also, being fined or paying a fine does not necessary get you out of trouble. The assessment of a civil fine will in no way act as a legal bar to the investigation, arrest, charging, or prosecution for any other violation of this Act. This means the fines assessed may only be the beginning of your legal troubles.

This Chapter Written By: Patrick T. Barone, J.D. / Barone Defense Firm

CHAPTER EIGHT

Michigan's Medical Marihuana Tracking Act

House Bill 4827 was the last of the bills introduced in 2016, and this entirely new bill led to the creation of a series of new statutes that address the need to track medical marijuana "from seed to sale." These new statutes are set forth in MCL § 333.27901 to MCL §333.27904. The collective common name for this series of new statutes is the "Marihuana Tracking Act." In this chapter, many of the major features of this new series of laws will be discussed.

Overview of the Marihuana Tracking Act

The Marihuana Tracking Act (MTA) allows LARA to establish a statewide cloud-based internet medical marijuana monitoring system. This system must use integrated tracking, inventory, and verification (as briefly discussed in Chapter 5). There are many reasons why a tracking system is necessary, and first among them is that medical marijuana, like all marijuana, remains as a "schedule one" drug at both the state and federal levels.

Medical marijuana is also kind of like a prescription drug, and all scheduled prescription drugs are tracked at both the federal and state levels. For example, Michigan's prescription monitoring program, formerly called MAPS, is used to track controlled substances, scheduled 2-5 drugs. It is used to prevent drug abuse and diversion of prescription drugs. On April 4th, 2017 the state of Michigan replaced the MAPS platform with PMP AWARxE. According to the provider's website, PMP AWARxE provides access to mandatory pharmacy reporting and offers secure accessibility to data across state lines. The prescription drug monitoring system is what Michigan's law makers had in mind when they drafted this part of the legislation. Other medical marijuana states also have seed to sale tracking systems[1].

According to the MTA, the phrase "statewide monitoring system" means an internet-based, statewide database established, implemented, and maintained directly or indirectly by LARA that is available to medical marijuana licensees, law enforcement agencies, and authorized state departments and agencies on a 24-hour basis. The system is used for many specific purposes, including verifying registry identification cards, tracking marijuana transfer, and transportation by licensees. In this regard, the system will track transferee's name, the date of transfer, the quantity, and price.

As part of the effort to prevent diversion and to ensure compliance with other aspects of the MMMA, the system will also be used to verify that a medical marijuana transfer will not exceed the limit that the registered qualifying patient or registered primary caregiver is authorized to receive by law[2].

Michigan's Medical Marihuana Tracking System

As indicated, the Department of Licensing and Regulatory Affairs (LARA) is required by the Marihuana Tracking Act to establish a cloud-based internet software system capable of effective monitoring of marijuana seed-to-sale transfers[3]. Accordingly, this system will be used to track, take inventory of, and verify marijuana. The system must be able to store and provide access to information that allows verification by a medical marijuana licensee that a patient or caregiver's registry identification card is current and valid and has not been suspended, revoked, or denied. Because of the need to ensure card-holder confidentiality, LARA is required to ensure that the software is capable of instituting procedures to ensure confidentiality by precluding the disclosure or use of information in the system for anything other than the enforcement, oversight, and implementation of the Michigan Medical Marihuana Act or the Medical Marihuana Facilities Licensing Act.

In addition, this tracking system must have the ability to interface with other, third-party systems. The description for these other tracking and inventory systems is defined in the Licensing Act. The system also must keep a record of quantity, date, time, and price of each transfer or sale of marijuana to a qualified patient or a caregiver, and verify that a sale or transfer will not exceed the limit established by MMMA[4].

Bids and Contracts for Tracking System

It is LARA's job to seek bids for the statewide tracking and monitoring system. LARA must evaluate bids in terms of both the cost of the service and the service's ability to meet the requirements of MMMA, the Licensing Act, and the Marihuana Tracking Act[5]. LARA also must consider the bidder's ability to prevent abuse, fraud, and other relevant issues that might arise when it comes to enforcing these Acts. The bidder must also not use the information in the system for purposes other than the oversight, implementation, and enforcement of the acts it applies to.

When LARA determines the appropriate system, the awardee must deliver the system within 180 days of the contract. A contract can be terminated if the awardee violates the Marihuana Tracking

Act. If this happens, the awardee could be barred from other contracts with the state.

The information within the tracking system must be confidential. It also must be exempt from disclosure under the Freedom of Information Act (FOIA). Information in the tracking system can only be disclosed to enforce the MMMA, the Marihuana Tracking Act, or the Medical Marihuana Facilities Licensing Act[6].

This Chapter Written By: Patrick T. Barone, J.D. / Barone Defense Firm

CHAPTER NINE

Beyond Licensing

How to Legally and Safely Possess, Process, Transport, and Sell Medical Marijuana in Michigan

If you started this book with some general questions about obtaining a medical marijuana related license with the hope of starting a new business, then I hope that most of your questions have been cleared up by now. This chapter will be devoted to a few of the common questions that clients come to me with, in case you still have some confusion or need information about your license. I will touch on the question of multiple licenses and other related licenses that you might want to apply for in this chapter.

Multiple Licenses

At this point, you should be aware that you cannot obtain all five of the available medical marijuana licenses. This is because the Medical Marihuana Facilities Licensing Act is designed to prevent one company from having too much market power. The Act is also designed to prevent fraud and diversion. For example, if you apply for a marijuana transporter's license, you cannot also obtain a marijuana processor license. This is because one requirement for the transporter license is that you or your company must not have a vested interest in other licenses or parts of the process.

This makes the medical marijuana business a symbiotic system. You cannot go through the whole process of growing, cultivating, testing, transporting, and selling medical marijuana on your own. Instead, your business will provide one, or sometimes more than one, part of the necessary services that make up the whole process. This means that you will have to be in contact with other businesses and vendors who take care of the processes that you do not have a license to cover. Depending on the mix of licenses you apply for, in some instances if you apply for multiple licenses, you will be denied on that basis alone. And, if you try to do aspects of the process that you are not licensed to do, you will be subject to sanctions.

Here is what is and is not allowed for each kind of license holder (licensee):

1. **Grower Licensee:** To be eligible for a grower license, the applicant and each investor in the grower must not have an interest in a secure transporter or safety compliance facility[1].
2. **Processor Licensee:** To be eligible for a processor license, the applicant and each investor in the processor must not have an interest in a secure transporter or safety compliance facility[2].
3. **Secure Transporter Licensee:** To be eligible for a secure transporter license, the applicant and each investor with an interest in the secure transporter must not have an interest in a grower, processor, provisioning center, or safety compliance facility and must not be a registered qualifying patient or a registered primary caregiver.
4. **Provisioning Licensee:** To be eligible for a provisioning center license, the applicant and each investor in the provisioning center must not have an interest in a secure transporter or safety compliance facility[3].
5. **Safety Compliance Facility Licensee:** To be eligible for a safety compliance facility license, the applicant and each investor with any interest in the safety compliance facility

must not have an interest in a grower, secure transporter, processor, or provisioning center[4].

By process of elimination then, here are the multiple licenses that may be held:

1. **Growers:** may also hold a processor license and/or a provisioning license.
2. **Processors:** may also hold a grower's license and/or a provisioning license.
3. **Secure Transporters:** cannot hold any other licenses.
4. **Provisioners:** may also hold a grower's license and/or a processing license.
5. **Safety Compliance Labs:** like transporters, they may not hold any other license.

A Note on Security

Unfortunately, it is the nature of the medical marijuana business that all licensees must carefully consider how to keep their businesses secure. This includes their physical facilities, data, and products. Other than background checks for licensees and their agents and employees, the three Acts discussed in this book do not address security in any way. This means it will be up to you to consult with law enforcement and private security companies to determine how to keep yourself, your employees, and your business safe. In this regard, you may wonder if you should keep a firearm at the business for self-defense purposes. You may also wonder if you should obtain a license to carry a concealed pistol. Both questions are answered below.

Your Right to Keep and Bear Arms

Both the United States Constitution and the Michigan constitution allow citizens to keep and bear arms. Article I, Section 6 reads:

> **§ 6 Bearing of arms.**
> **Sec. 6.** Every person has a right to keep and bear arms for the defense of himself and the state[5].

Unlike the Second Amendment of the United States Constitution, this section of the Michigan constitution specifically provides that Michigan citizens have a right to self-defense. However, like the United States Supreme Court, Michigan Courts have held that this right is not unlimited, meaning it's subject to reasonable limitations[6].

Use of Firearms in Self-Defense

In Michigan, you have a right to keep a firearm in your home or business and no license or permit is necessary. However, even when lawful, using your weapon in self-defense is fraught with risk and legal complications. If you intend to keep a weapon at your medical marijuana related business, then it is essential for you to become knowledgeable on applicable Michigan law. It is impossible to cover the breadth of this law in this book. Readers interested in learning more are encouraged to obtain a copy of Mr. Barone's book entitled *Michigan Gun Law* (currently in print). This 400+ page book covers all aspects of firearm ownership and use.

Generally, you may not use deadly force to protect property in Michigan. Thus, your weapon should only be used for the defense of yourself and others. The primary self-defense statute in Michigan Penal Code lays out the legal requirement for the justified use of deadly force for self-defense[7]. This section establishes that a person is legally justified in using deadly force to protect him or herself or another person, with no duty to retreat, provided:

- They're not engaged in a crime;
- They're in a place they have a right to be;
- They honestly and reasonably believe that deadly force is necessary;
- They are preventing imminent death, great bodily harm, or sexual assault to themselves or others.

The word "crime" is extremely broad and could theoretically encompass many activities not related to the act of self-defense. Please note also that neither the MMMA, MMLFA or the MTA specifically provide legal protections for the use of firearms. Also, as discussed in prior chapters, possessing, processing, transporting, selling, and using marijuana remains illegal at the federal level. Consequently, mixing firearm possession or use with medical marijuana encompasses considerable risk.

Also, as you can see from the above, to lawfully use a weapon in self-defense you must reasonably believe it is necessary. It could be up to a police officer or prosecutor to decide if your use was reasonable. However, if you are using the weapon in Michigan, there is a statute that reads: "it is a rebuttable presumption in a civil or criminal case that an individual who uses deadly force or force other than deadly force has an honest and reasonable belief (fill in the appropriate circumstances: *e.g.*, prevent murder, sexual assault, *etc.*) will occur."[8] The rebuttable presumption only applies when the force or deadly force is used inside a home or business. If a person is in fear of imminent death, serious injury, or sexual assault outside a home or business, then they may still use deadly or non-deadly force but *they are not protected* by the presumption. Again, a detailed analysis of this presumption, and the overall use of force in Michigan is beyond the scope of this book. These topics are also discussed in detail in Mr. Barone's compendium on these issues entitled *Michigan Gun Law*.

Conflict Between Your Right to Bear Arms and Your Right to Lawfully Use Medical Marijuana

The conflicts between state and federal law described in Chapter 3 also come into play as they relate to the use of medical marijuana. Many believe that this conflict of laws means that a person who obtains a medical marijuana card is precluded from owning a weapon and/or obtaining a concealed pistol license. This is because a federal law specifically makes it unlawful for any person who is an unlawful user of or addicted to any controlled substance (as defined in section 102 of the Controlled Substances Act)[9], "to ship or transport in interstate or foreign commerce, or possess in or affecting commerce, any firearm or ammunition; or to receive any firearm or ammunition which has been shipped or transported in interstate or foreign commerce."[10]

Furthermore, in an "open letter" dated September 21, 2011 and written by Arthur Herbert, Assistant Director of the Enforcement Programs and Services of the US Department of Justice, BATF, and directed to "all federal firearms licensees," indicates that, "there are no exceptions in Federal law for marijuana purportedly used for medical purposes, even when sanctioned by State law." Furthermore, the letter indicates that it is unlawful for a person addicted to marijuana to possess either firearms or ammunition. Finally, the letter indicates that federal firearms licensee's may not transfer firearms or ammunition to a person they know or have reasonable cause to believe may be an unlawful user of or addicted to marijuana. This is true even if the person attempting to obtain a firearm or ammunition answers "no" to this question on their Firearms Transaction Record[11].

However, concealed pistol licenses (CPL) are governed by Michigan state law and not by federal law, and there is no specific preclusion for medical marijuana licensees under state law. Consequently, whether a medical marijuana card holder may simultaneously hold a CPL remains an open question that has not yet been litigated. One state that has litigated this issue, or one close to it, is Oregon, whose Supreme Court has indicated[12] that state sheriffs had a duty under state concealed handgun licensing law, to issue concealed carry permits to qualified applicants without regard to their use of medical marijuana. The court also held that this duty was not preempted by the Federal Gun Control Act of 1968's prohibition on possession of firearms by unlawful users of controlled substances. Finally, the court indicated that state sheriff's failure to issue concealed carry licenses was not excused because such issuance to a medical marijuana user would violate the section of federal act prohibiting the making of any statement that is likely to deceive a gun dealer regarding the lawfulness of the sale of a firearm.

In considering the interplay between these two rights, you are well advised to know that by possessing both a CPL and/or a firearm, you may be in violation of federal law, and you may be precluded for purchasing or possessing a firearm.

Also, it is worth noting that many medical marijuana entrepreneurs will not be medical marijuana patients and will not be users of marijuana. Consequently, the question of whether you may co-own a medical marijuana business license is a little bit different, and it seems more likely that there is no conflict between the two. However, your best bet is to leave the armed protection up to police officers and licensed security companies and their personnel.

Concealed Pistol License Requirements

The above discussion regarding the inadvisability of combining firearms and marijuana, notwithstanding, Michigan is considered a "shall issue" state, meaning unless you are otherwise precluded by law, and provided you've met certain minimal requirements, you are entitled to a concealed pistol license (CPL)[13]. However, before filing your application for a CPL, you should make sure that you meet certain requirements. For example, you must be at least 21 years old and either a United States citizen or a lawfully admitted alien.

In addition, you need to be a current resident of the state of Michigan, and you must live there for at least six months before you apply for the CPL. It is relatively easy to prove residency. For example, a valid driver's license or state ID will be sufficient. Applicants that are on active duty with the Armed Services are also able to obtain a CPL in Michigan if Michigan remains their home of record while stationed outside of the state. Alternatively, they could get a CPL in Michigan if they are stationed in Michigan but permanently reside elsewhere.

There are also a few instances where a county clerk can waive the six-month residency requirement. For example, this might occur in the case of an emergency license, where the applicant is a petitioner for a personal protection order[14]. An emergency license can also be requested if a county sheriff determines that there is convincing and clear evidence that the safety of the applicant or a member of the applicant's family will be in immediate danger. Finally, if you are a new resident in Michigan and you hold a CPL from another state, the six-month residency requirement can be waived.

In addition to the residency requirement, the state of Michigan wants to make sure that you know how to safely handle and use a pistol before they grant a CPL. To make sure that you have this training, you must complete a pistol safety training class or course.

Another requirement is that you have not faced a disposition or order for certain issues. This includes involuntary treatment or hospitalization, legal incapacitation, finding of not guilty by insanity in a case, a bond, or conditional release that prohibits possession or purchase of a firearm, or a personal protection order. If you face one or more of these issues, you will not be eligible for a CPL.

Additionally, a prior conviction for, or having a currently pending crime, will also mean you will be prohibited from using, possessing, transporting, selling, carrying, purchasing, distributing, shipping, or receiving a firearm[15]. For example, many of the convictions that you may not have in the past or have currently pending are driving related. If you have these crimes pending, or have been convicted, then you won't qualify for a CPL. First, you cannot be convicted of or face conviction for failing to stop if you are involved in a personal injury accident[16]. You also can't be convicted of operating a motor vehicle while intoxicated or under the influence of cocaine or a "schedule 1" controlled substance, including marijuana[17]. Similarly, you can't be convicted of operating a commercial motor vehicle while under the influence of alcohol[18]. You can't be convicted of reckless driving or driving with a revoked or suspended license if you want to apply for a CPL.

Just as you should not be convicted of crimes involving a car if you want to apply for a CPL, you also shouldn't be convicted of operating an aircraft while under the influence of alcohol or a controlled substance. A conviction for operating a vessel under the influence of alcohol or a controlled substance will also disqualify you from getting a CPL[19]. The same goes for operating an off-road vehicle or a snowmobile under the influence of alcohol or a controlled substance.

Other disqualifying convictions deal with assault. For example, assault or domestic assault, aggravated assault or aggravated domestic assault, or showing sexually explicit material to minors. Other violent crimes that will make you ineligible include vulnerable adult abuse, fourth degree child abuse, indecent exposure, stalking and fourth degree criminal sexual conduct.

Many other convictions that will make you ineligible for a CPL are related to firearms. For example, illegal sale of ammunition or a firearm, improper possession or transportation of a loaded firearm in a motor vehicle, or failure to register a purchased firearm component or firearm. Another issue is obtaining a pistol in an improper manner, making a false statement on the application to buy a pistol, or attempting to use or using someone else's identification to buy a pistol.

Other firearm related crimes include intentionally aiming or pointing a firearm without malice, discharging a firearm while it is intentionally aimed without malice, possessing a firearm in a prohibited area, brandishing a firearm while you are in public, and possessing a firearm in public if you are less than 18 years old. Additional crimes include discharging a firearm aimed or pointed intentionally without malice but causing injury, setting a trap, device, spring, or other gun, or possessing, carrying, using, or discharging a firearm if you are under the influence of alcohol or a controlled substance. This list is non-exhaustive, and readers interested in knowing more are encouraged to consult *Michigan Gun Law.*

You can't be convicted of a crime listed above within eight years of applying for a pistol license. In addition to these crimes, there are crimes which you cannot be convicted of within three years before you apply for the license. Along with not being convicted of these crimes that are mentioned, if you have been dishonorably discharged from the Armed Services, you will not qualify for a CPL. When you apply for a CPL, it is also important that you do not have a felony charge pending against you. The state considers this a disqualification for a CPL. In addition, you will not be eligible if you have ever been convicted of a felony in a state other than Michigan.

There are also many provisions related to mental illness. You cannot be found not guilty or acquitted of any crime due to mental illness or insanity. In addition, you cannot currently be or in the past have been involuntarily committed to an inpatient or outpatient organization because of mental illness. Also, you cannot have a diagnosis of mental illness at the time of your application that states that you are a danger to yourself or other people, whether you are receiving treatment for a mental illness or not. You cannot be under a legal incapacity court order in Michigan or any other state. Finally, you must have a valid personal identification card, such as a state issued driver's license.

The above lists the state requirements for CPL eligibility. In addition, you need to consider federal requirements. The only federal requirement for a CPL is that those prohibited from transporting or possessing a firearm determined by the federal National Instant Criminal Background Check System (NICS) do not qualify. If you have questions, contact the NICS section of the FBI. They can be reached at 1-877-324-6427.

Preparing and filing your CPL application is intended to be a "do it yourself" endeavor. More information is available on the internet. This topic is also discussed in detail in *Michigan Gun Law*.

A Note on Operating a Pistol Under the Influence of Medical Marijuana

Michigan's laws related to firearms provide that an individual "shall not carry a concealed pistol while he or she is under the influence of alcoholic liquor or a controlled substance or while having a bodily alcohol content prohibited under this section[20]." This is like the way intoxicated driving is defined in Michigan's motor vehicle code because a person violates the law when they are either "under the influence" or have an "unlawful bodily alcohol content." This mimics the OUIL/UBAL paradigm in the motor vehicle code.

However, unlike the motor vehicle code, the phrase "under the influence" related to firearm possession or use is defined by statute. According to law, "under the influence of alcoholic liquor or a controlled substance[21]" means that the individual's ability to properly handle a pistol or to exercise clear judgment regarding the use of that pistol was substantially and materially affected by the consumption of alcoholic liquor or a controlled substance.

This is a higher standard than that suggested by case law under the motor vehicle code. Presumably "under the Influence" not supported by chemical evidence could be proved using the observations of the police office, including such things as slurred speech and poor performance on field sobriety tasks. Again, for a more detailed discussion of "observation evidence" please refer to the prior chapter.

This Chapter Written By: Patrick T. Barone, J.D. / Barone Defense Firm

CHAPTER TEN

Michigan Business Forms

Applying for a medical marijuana business license is one thing, but getting a business approved in Michigan is another. Before you continue with your plans of running a marijuana growing business or opening a medical marijuana dispensary, you need to familiarize yourself with Michigan laws for starting and running a business. Throughout this process, you may want to work with an attorney in order to understand business organization, important parts of a business plan, following laws related to businesses, and more. I will discuss these steps in the process in this chapter, as well as other important aspects of starting and running a business.

Should You Start a Business?

Before you jump in, it is important to make sure that you are ready to begin your own business. Owning your business can be a great experience, but it also comes with a lot of stress and responsibility. You need to make sure that you are ready for this challenge before you begin the process.

There are a lot of questions that you should ask yourself before beginning your own business. By determining why you want to start your own business, recognizing your personal strengths and weaknesses, and determining your business goals, you can make this process easier. Review the following topics carefully to determine if you are ready to start your own business.

The first thing that you want to do is determine why you want to start your own business. Ask yourself what you hope to get out of the business and why you need to create your own business in order to achieve these goals. Then, you should consider the specific type of business that you want to begin. This answer will likely coincide with what type of license you are applying for.

You should also think about how you will make this business work. What makes you believe that you can run a sustainable and successful business? What kind of skills or experience do you have in this industry? What can you bring to the business (what are your strengths)? What will you need help with (what are your weaknesses)? These are important things to consider.

You also need to think about finances. What are your financial goals for the business? Can you fund this project on your own? Will you need financial assistance, and if so, where will this help come from? Do you have the credit and the resources to get financial help?

Once you get a business running, you need to be able to sustain it. This can mean working in a high stress environment. On the one hand, you are your own boss, which gives you some freedom. But, you are also responsible for your employees and your products. This means that a lot of work will fall on your shoulders. Can your emotional and mental health take this stress? Do you have the stamina to succeed? How will you balance your work and your personal life? How will you manage your employees and the business day in and day out?

These are all important topics to consider and questions to ask yourself before proceeding. Putting the effort in now to think this through can help you prepare for the future and ensure that you run a successful business.

Business Structures

If you have determined that starting a business is right for you, the next thing to consider is the business structure you want to utilize. Understanding the various business structures available to you can help you choose the right one.

The main business structure choices to consider are a sole proprietor, a corporation, a partnership, or an LLC. When determining the best structure for you, you should consider investment needs, income taxes, liabilities and risks of your business, and the expenses and formalities involved in that structure. Below, I will discuss each of these business structures.

The sole proprietorship is a common form of small business that has one owner. This is the default for a small business, because it does not require any paperwork to set up. If you are interested in a sole proprietorship, but you don't want to use your personal name, you can apply for a sole proprietorship "doing business as" (DBA). You can get a certificate for this form of proprietorship from a county clerk.

In a sole proprietorship or sole proprietorship DBA, there isn't a legal separation between an owner of the business and the business itself. This means that you take on the full responsibility of the debts and liabilities involved with the business. If you cannot pay, a vendor can sue you individually, leaving you little protection. In addition, losses or income from the business are listed on your personal tax return.

A few advantages of the sole proprietorship are that they are easy to set up and they are inexpensive. In addition, profits are taxed once at the owner's rate. But, you also need to consider the disadvantages. In this business structure, you personally have unlimited liability for the business' debts. Also, you can only establish one person as the owner of the business.

If you want to establish a business that is separate from you, consider a corporation. Corporations are legal entities that are separate from any members or owners. The business itself has its own liabilities, privileges, and rights. Owners of the business, including stockholders and shareholders, do not take on the business' debts as their personal responsibility. Corporations can have one owner or multiple owners. Generally, shareholders of the corporation elect a Board of Directors. This board makes major decisions and oversees policies. They also hire employees to oversee the business from day to day. The corporation itself can be sued or sue, own property, and enter into contracts.

Of all the business structures, a corporation is the most complex and expensive to establish. You need to file Articles of Incorporation with LARA and pay the application fees. There is also an annual fee that needs to go to LARA. Corporations also need to comply with many different formalities in order to stay in business, so running them can be a complex process. Also consider that corporations pay taxes at special rates, so they are subject to double taxation. This can be avoided by applying for the subchapter S corporation, but not all corporations are eligible for this.

Overall, some advantages of starting a corporation include the ease of transferring ownership and the ease of raising capital through stock. In addition, you might be able to get a subchapter S with the IRS. Finally, there is limited liability for the business' debts, which protects shareholders. It is also important to consider the disadvantages. First, corporations can be expensive to set up and maintain. Also, it can be difficult to maintain corporations, as there are a lot of regulations to follow. Corporations are also closely regulated by the government. Finally, if your corporation is not eligible for subchapter S, it can be subject to double taxation.

Another business structure option that you have is a partnership. There are two main types of partnership that you can consider - the general partnership and the limited partnership. In some ways, the general partnership is similar to a sole proprietorship. One major difference is that a general partnership can have more than one owner. There is no paperwork to fill out or anything that you need to do in order to set up a general partnership, just like a sole proprietorship.

Like the sole proprietorship, you can use your own name or set up a partnership under a different name if you apply for a DBA certificate with a county clerk.

If you have more than one partner in the partnership, it is a good idea to establish a partnership agreement. This agreement can address any possible issues that might arise, the role of each partner, and any other important information. This can avoid disagreements in the future. Owners of general partnerships have unlimited liability when it comes to business debts. Each partner is responsible for the debt that the business takes on.

If you are looking into a partnership, you should also consider the limited partnership option. This type of partnership can have both general and limited partners. General partners are completely liable for the business' debts. They are also responsible for operating and controlling the business. Limited partners, on the other hand, are usually investors in the business. They are not responsible for controlling or operating the business. In addition, their personal liability in the business is limited to their contribution to the partnership.

Establishing a limited partnership in Michigan requires filing a certificate of limited partnership with LARA. Limited partnerships that don't comply with regulations default to general partnerships.

Again, there are many different advantages and disadvantages of the partnership option. Some advantages include the ease and lack of expense to set them up, a single tax, and ownership by more than one person. Some disadvantages are unlimited personal liability for general partners, legal responsibility of each partner for the actions of one partner, and the fact that a general partner's interest in the business can only be sold with the consent of all partners.

LLC stands for limited liability company. LLCs combine the best aspects of corporations and partnerships. An LLC provides the owners or partners in the business limited liability when it comes to business debt. In addition, it establishes simpler taxing and operation advantages than a partnership would offer.

If you are interested in applying for an LLC, it is a good idea to file an operating agreement, although one is not required in the state of Michigan. Still, it is a good idea to establish such an agreement in order to outline expectations and responsibilities of members. Even if you don't file an operating agreement, you do need to file the Articles of Organization with LARA. You also have to pay an annual fee if you want to maintain an LLC.

Some advantages of the LLC are limited liability for partners, no double taxation, and ease to create and maintain. Some disadvantages of the LLC are that it is more complex to create than some other options, members can only take money out through profit distribution, and members are not exempt from paying self-employment taxes.

Steps in Creating a Business

Once you determine that you do want to start your own business, and figure out the business structure that you want to work with, it's time to create the business! Here, I will discuss the various steps involved in establishing your business.

Step One: Establish Your Business Idea

In order to move forward, it is important to have a firm understanding of what you want your business to do. What problems will your business solve? How? If you are unsure how to answer these questions, don't worry. Step two can help!

Step Two: Conduct Market Research

Early on in the process, you should conduct market research to determine if your business and business plan are feasible. In other words, you need to make sure that your business is doable. Market research can help you determine the direction to take with your business, what will be profitable, and more. A few major types of research include industry, market, customer, and competition research.

Industry research will provide you with an overall view of what is happening in your type of business, best practices, and some things that you should include in your business. Market research will help you determine businesses or consumers that will buy your service or product. Understanding market behaviors and patterns can help you focus your business. Market research is similar to customer research in that you are determining who will buy your service or product. Customer research is a little more specific. You want to figure out who will be interested in your services and how to reach them. Also consider researching your competitors. Find businesses in your industry and see what they do well. Also consider what they do poorly, so that your business can do that better.

Two common ways to do market research are using the internet or going to a library. Search engines can help you find much of what you are looking for without leaving the comfort of your home. You can conduct this research at night or on the weekends.

It can also be worthwhile to check out a library and do some research there. Many libraries have business librarians who can assist you with the process and answer any questions that you have. You can also find useful information in books that the library provides. Consider searching through books such as the *Directory of Trade Associations, the Economic Census*, the *Encyclopedia of American Industries*, the *Encyclopedia of Global Industries*, government surveys, and industry publications.

Step Three: Establish Your Startup Cost

Having a solid concept of costs before you begin your business can mean the difference between succeeding and failing. Before starting, it is important to do an in-depth cost analysis in order to make realistic estimates of what the business will cost. Common issues such as startup loans, resources, grants, unrealistic estimated profits, and more can mean a lot of stress and difficulty in getting your business off the ground. Thinking about these costs before you begin can be helpful. Here are a few startup costs to consider to get you started.

First, you need to think about property costs. Think about costs for down payments on property, closing costs, utility deposits, remodeling costs, and more. Then, consider the equipment that you will need to run your business. This might include furniture, vehicles, signs, computers, telecommunication equipment, fixtures, production equipment and machinery, and more. Next, think about the materials and supplies that your business might need. This could include production materials, office supplies, and your starting inventory. If you want to market your business, you need to allocate money for this. Consider the money you will need for advertising, promotional items, and marketing consultants. You should also think about operational expenses and fees. You might need trade association memberships, permits, licenses, patent or trademark fees, professional fees for accountants, lawyers, etc., or insurance. Also think about your personal living expenses. How will you survive from the time that you get your last paycheck at your old job to the time that you open your new business? How will you survive in the first few months when the business is just getting off the ground? You also need to consider working capital and your cash reserve. Allocate money for salaries, wages, opening expenses, and more.

After you do this in-depth cost analysis, you need to figure out where the money for starting your business will come from. How much money will you and your family put up for the business? If this is not enough to get the business going, you should consider options such as grants, loans, and crowdfunding to help with the costs.

Another option is taking out a loan. There are a few factors that you need to consider before applying for a loan. First, you need to consider your character and how a lender will view it. Consider your credit score and your credit history in the past 3-5 years. A lender will also consider the cash that you can put into the business. A lender will expect you to put up 20-30% of startup costs. If you do get a loan, you might be expected to put up collateral for the loan. Make sure that you have the ability to do this. Also, loans to the medical marijuana industry are likely going to be more difficult to obtain, especially at first, since marijuana remains illegal at the federal level.

In addition, you could crowdfund. This is a way to get loans or support for your business by networking and contacting interested parties. This is a relatively new form of building capital for your business, so if you want to consider this option, you should contact an attorney to make sure that you follow federal rules that apply.

Once you consider how much it will cost to start and run your business, as well as what kind of capital you have available to you, you need to decide if your business is feasible. Can you realistically make the business work from a financial perspective? If you can, continue to step four. If not, you might need to reconsider your plan.

Step Four: Write Your Business Plan

Lack of planning is one of the main reasons why new small businesses fail. To avoid this issue, it is important that you take the time to conduct research, organize your business model, and create an actionable plan. This will take the form of a business plan.

A written business plan can have many benefits. First, this plan can help you immensely as you navigate the business owning process. Of course, you have a general idea of your business in your head, but putting pen to paper can help you generate new ideas, take note of the gaps in your plan, and articulate your ideas. Instead of trying to remember every detail, writing it out and analyzing your research can keep you organized and give you a good idea of what is next.

In addition, writing a business plan gives you the opportunity to test out financial scenarios, review the economic environment, determine your market, plan out your operations, and more, before you invest money into the project. You can consider various different situations, determine what will and will not work, and adjust before investing in the business to make sure it is successful.

Beyond helping you plan the business, a business plan can help you financially. This is because many lenders and investors want to see a written plan. They want to know exactly what they are investing in before they jump in. A business plan will provide the foundation for a financial plan that lenders and investors oftentimes require. This plan can mean the difference between hooking investors and getting a loan, and walking away empty handed.

While there is no exact formula for creating a business plan, there are sample business plans and outlines that you can refer to online. Below I will discuss some general sections to consider adding to your business plan to get you started with this process.

You want to begin your business plan by organizing and introducing the content itself. Start with a cover page that states the name of your business, as well as the names and contact information for the principals involved. Then, you want to create a table of contents so that those reading the business plan can easily access different sections. Next, you should create a brief summary explaining the major elements of your business plan. This only needs to be a page or two, but it can be used as a stand-alone document when sharing the plan with others. For those who do not have the time to read everything, they can get the main points from the summary. Although the summary should come towards the beginning of the document, you should write it last, once you have made all of the decisions that need to go into your business plan.

After these initial sections, you should provide a company introduction. You might express an overview of your company, its mission statement, company history, your services or products, legal structure, and more.

Once you introduce your company, you should provide a section on sales and marketing. Your marketing research can go in this section. Include your industry and market analysis here. You can also provide information about your competitors and your customers. You should also establish your marketing and sales plan, which might include value proposition, strategic partners, advertising, customer service, distribution, and more.

The next section in the business plan should be your management and operations section. Here, you will discuss how the business will be organized and run from day-to-day. Express information about your management team, other important personnel, your staff and your objectives for them, the budget you have allocated for human resources, information about the Directors or the Board involved in the company, and the business' work process. Information about company inventory, quality control, production, subcontractors, equipment, facilities, and more can go here.

Another section that your business plan should have is one regarding financials. Provide information about startup costs and establish realistic financial projections, especially for the first few years. Your projections should include income, expenses, and cash flow.

After these main sections, you can provide an appendix if there are additional documents that you want to attach to your business plan. Any forms or documents that you reference within the plan should be provided here. This might include personal financial statements, purchase settlements, employee resumes, site plans, tax returns, and more.

For assistance writing your business plan, there are many online resources that you can refer to. If you want more help, contacting a lawyer is a good idea.

Step Five: Establishing Your Business Management Team

Everyone has strengths and weaknesses, and it is important to consider what you can and cannot bring to your business. The good news is that for areas that you have gaps or a lack of proficiency, you can find other people who excel. Putting together a diverse team will ensure that your business has someone who can handle every aspect of the business. Consider some positions that you will need to fill at your business, such as an accountant or bookkeeper, a lawyer, an insurance agent, specialized consultants, a realtor, a staffing service, and IT services consultants. Building a strong team will help your business succeed.

Step Six: Make Sure You are Ready to Open

At some point before you open your business, there are many legal tasks that you need to complete. Some of these tasks might be completed as first steps, while others can wait until later on in the process. But, before you can finalize your business, you need to consider and complete the following tasks.

One basic task to complete before finalizing your business is choosing a business structure and choosing a name for the business. Once this is done, there are some legal aspects to consider. For example, if you need a specific license to run a business, make sure that you obtain this. If your business structure requires registration at the state and/or federal level, make sure that you do this. You will also have to establish tax registration at the state and federal levels.

You as the employer or the business itself also need to obtain a taxpayer identification number. Your business might require an employer identification number (EIN), so it is important to look into this. If your business contains a copyright, trademark, or patent, you should also look into intellectual property (IP) identification. Along the same lines is how you will present your company through imaging and branding. Come up with a branding strategy and make sure that you can legally do what you want to do before implementing this strategy. Many of these topics are considered in greater detail in Chapter 12.

Before finalizing your business, establishing business insurance can be helpful. You should talk with an insurance agent to discuss the type(s) of insurance that will be useful for your business to have. Insurance rates and options will vary, so do some research before settling on what you buy and where you get it from.

Hiring employees is another aspect that you need to give thought to. Make sure that your employees are qualified and that they can handle responsibilities at both the state and the federal levels.

Especially for a business related to medical marijuana, it is important to review local and zoning requirements. Make sure that the place that you plan on setting up your business complies with local regulations and laws.

Finally, if you are thinking about buying an existing business, you need to make sure that you have the ability to make an informed decision. This requires extensive financial and operational information from the seller. You should contact an attorney to review your contracts and situation before purchasing an existing business.

Step Seven: Start Your Business!

Once you complete the steps outlined above, you are ready to begin your business.

This is just a basic outline for starting a business. If you need more information about this process, please read Chapter 11. You may also wish to consult with a business lawyer to assist you with your business planning and the writing of your business plan.

This Chapter Written By: Patrick T. Barone, J.D. / Barone Defense Firm

CHAPTER ELEVEN

Incorporating
Forming and Managing the "Going Concern" of Your Business

In the previous chapter, I discussed some possible business formations that you might explore if setting up a business related to medical marijuana. In this chapter, I will discuss these options in greater detail.

A number of methods and best practices exist for anyone to do business in their respective state, all of which are legal, but not all of which provide the maximum protection of shareholders' and /or members' personal assets and corporate assets. The field of medical marijuana is no different than any other business, notwithstanding the specifically regulated nature of the business, and that it involves agriculturally based services/products. The purpose of this chapter is to identify key issues for a new business owner as to the utilization and purpose of statutorily authorized business entities.

The corporation is a common form of business entity used for the organization and operation of a small business, although the limited liability company (LLC) has become more popular in recent years.

Forming the Corporation/ Limited Liability Company

Corporations

A corporation is fairly easy and inexpensive to form. The corporate entity affords its owners protection from personal liability for the debts and obligations of the business and may make favorable pass-through tax treatment available under the federal tax laws (subchapter S). The ownership interests of a corporate entity are generally freely transferable. Although corporations require that certain formalities be observed (e.g., actions by the board of directors and shareholders must be taken at meetings or by written consent and records of the action must be maintained) and have been viewed as less flexible than other business entities (like partnerships and LLCs) in allowing different treatment among investors, amendments to the Michigan Business Corporation Act (MBCA) have significantly reduced these differences for nonpublic profit corporations.

A corporation, like a partnership and an LLC, is a creature of statute. Each state, like Michigan, has its own corporate statute that governs the formation, capitalization, management, business combination, and dissolution of corporations organized within the state. The statutes also govern the licensing or qualification of foreign corporations doing business in the state.

In Michigan, the statute is the MBCA, MCL 450.1101 et seq. The MBCA governs Michigan profit corporations. The formation of certain other kinds of corporations are governed by other Michigan statutes.

In Michigan, a corporation is formed by the filing of Articles of Incorporation (articles) with the Department of Licensing and Regulatory Affairs (LARA), and the payment of necessary filing fees. The principal documents for the organization of a corporation include the articles, bylaws, share certificates, and organizational minutes or written consents. Shareholder agreements among the corporation and shareholders are common.

The owners of a corporation are its shareholders. The ownership interests are shares. A corporation is managed by its board of directors, who are elected by the shareholders and who owe fiduciary duties of care and loyalty to the shareholders. The officers are appointed by the board of directors and have the authority specified by the board and/or the bylaws of the corporation. The principal attributes of a corporation are perpetual life, limited liability, centralized management, and free transferability of ownership interests.

Limited Liability Companies

Since 1983, the state of Michigan statutorily authorized the Michigan Limited Liability Company Act (LLCs), which was based on the act originally developed in the state of Delaware. After much tinkering, the state of Michigan returned to a draft of the act which virtually mirrored the Delaware Act. This changed corporate law in Michigan forever because the act authorized the existence and use of limited liability companies.

Limited liability companies are different than corporations (either IRS subchapter C or S corporations) in the following key ways: 1) Parties in LLCs are called "members" and parties in corporations are called "shareholders"; 2) LLCs are flow-through taxable entities whereby each member's income is taxed, once, at their personal rate only; 3) LLCs convey limited liability to each member of the LLC without requiring rigorous adherence to complying with the corporate form of entity maintenance, including but not limited to, conducting annual meetings, maintenance of a corporate minute/record book, issuance of formal corporate resolutions, and the like. Accordingly, the LLC is an extremely flexible corporate entity that has revolutionized the use of limited liability companies in all areas of commerce.

Formation of a limited liability company in support of any medical marijuana enterprise should be seriously considered, in that it is simply too easy not to do so; forming of an LLC with the state of Michigan through the Department of Licensing and Regulatory Affairs (LARA) is a simple process, performed online, that does not necessarily require legal counsel, although such counsel invariably will be very helpful. Fees associated with such formation are nominal, at several hundred dollars in filing fees at most. In return, each member of a limited liability company achieves limited personal liability in connection with the operations of the company (excepting personal acts—see more below), thereby safe-guarding other personal assets gained outside of or as a result of the operations of the business.

This is not to denigrate or lessen the importance of non-LLC corporate entities, either a subchapter C or S corporation, and in fact such entities may be more advisable for a particular medical marijuana enterprise, especially one that contemplates acquiring a large amount of manufacturing equipment requiring depreciation (or other tax treatment) that may be more favorable under these corporate forms. Each venture needs to review their contemplated operations with capital requirements and tax implications of same, as part of the determination of how to incorporate. Be that as it may, the limited liability company may be the entity of choice for most medical marijuana ventures, for the reasons mentioned, among others. There are multiple other manners in which to operate business ventures, partnerships, sole proprietorships, etc. but none of these offer the limited liability that is provided by the LLC entity, combined with the flexibility of maintenance of the corporate form.

The first question that should be asked is whether the LLC is the appropriate form of business entity. To answer this question, an attorney, along with the business organizers, should consider both the business goals of the organizers as a group and the personal relationships among them. The attorney may also help the organizers identify the corporate characteristics that are important to them. Are the limited liability and automatic pass-through tax characteristics of an LLC important? Is the flexibility of the LLC important (including being able to freely choose among the characteristics of centralized management, continuity of life, and free transferability)? Or are the automatic characteristics of limited liability, centralized management, continuity of life, and the elective pass-through tax status of an S corporation more important? While the LLC would appear to be the entity of choice for a closely held medical marijuana venture, one should not choose the LLC without considering other entity options.

A subchapter S corporation is a viable alternative because it accomplishes the goals of limited liability, flexibility, and pass-through taxation. Moreover, shareholders in an S corporation are not subject to self-employment tax, while members of an LLC may be. You must always consult with your tax representative (CPA or counsel) in this regard.

Operating/Governing Your Entity

Corporations have a contract among its shareholders called "bylaws" and an LLC has a contract among its members sometimes called a "membership operating agreement." For all practical purposes they are one in the same. These contracts are the agreed upon rules governing operations of the business and can include or not include virtually any term the members or shareholders can think of and wish to treat in such a contract.

The Michigan Limited Liability Company Act does not require LLCs to have an operating agreement. However, in practice, an operating agreement should almost always be used. A single-member LLC can now also have an operating agreement, and should, merely to demonstrate further compliance with the corporate form, further enhancing limited liability of the member. In practice, single-member LLCs may find it necessary to have a governing document of some kind because those who do business with the LLC may expect (or require) some written document that evidences the power and authority of the LLC and its member (and managers) to act.

Details of the LLC's organization, capital structure, governance, and operations must be worked out early on and should be provided for in a carefully drafted operating agreement. The operating agreement may also be used to modify the Michigan Limited

Liability Acts' various default rules (rules that will apply as a matter of statute in the event an operating agreement does not exist). Choices will have to be made about what default rules, if any, to modify and how to modify them. Almost invariably, LLC members will want to consult legal counsel who will be able to identify key issues that should be attended to in a final draft of an operating agreement.

Limited Liability

The hallmark of electing to form a limited liability company or a corporation is the maintenance of limited liability in your activities as a company or corporation. The usual push and pull is, if you have chosen limited liability for the business entity, you will not want to jeopardize it. At the same time, you will not want to bother with unnecessary notices of meetings, waivers of notices, drafting and redrafting of minutes, and so on.

Limited liability in this context means that entity owners and agents are not personally liable for entity obligations. It is inaccurate to suggest that forming a corporation or an LLC creates limited liability for its owners. Formation, by filing Articles of Formation (corporation) or organization (LLC), merely gives the owners the opportunity to have limited liability so long as the entity is operated with sufficient attention to keep it separate from its owners. Destroying this corporate limited liability shield is commonly referred to as "piercing the corporate veil." In the end, the factors bearing on corporate veil-piercing (getting to the finances of principals and destroying limited liability) are all entirely within the owners' control. All of those factors relate to how the owners have acted after the entity's articles were filed. While filing articles creates a limited liability shield, it is the owners' responsibility to maintain the shield.

Limited liability does not protect against an owner's personal negligence. Individuals remain responsible for direct liability. For example, licensed engineers would be personally liable for their negligence, even if they were acting on behalf of a corporate or an LLC employer. Nor would limited liability protect an owner from liability for negligent supervision of others. If an accident occurs and your owner or agent client was not personally on the job site, the likelihood of a negligent supervision claim against your client personally is greatly reduced. In that case, operating the business in a corporate or an LLC format would protect a principal's personal assets. If a principal is personally active in the business and there is a significant risk of tort liability from the owner's actions, however, operating in a limited liability entity may not provide much protection.

Liability for personal negligence exists regardless of whether the action was taken on the entity's behalf or was within the scope of that actor's employment. There is no requirement that a plaintiff "pierce the corporate veil" to hold corporate officials liable for their own tortious misconduct.

Limited liability does not protect an owner from that owner's personal contractual promises. An individual officer or shareholder is liable for the corporation's obligations only if that person signs individually on their own personal behalf, and this can be indicated where the person signs twice, once as an officer and once as an individual.

Having stated the above, maintaining the corporate form under the Michigan Limited Liability Act, and thus, safeguarding limited liability generally presents as a much more straightforward task, than other entities. Thus, this is one of the reasons that more and more business entities have turned to the LLC as the entity of choice. Of course, consultation with versed legal counsel, who can account for and assist business owners in categorizing the relative strengths and weaknesses of choice of entity, is paramount for any start-up commercial enterprise.

Best Practices: Maintenance of Limited Liability

As summarized above, and generally speaking, organizing and operating as an LLC affords a much more simplistic regimen and routine of daily operation relating to maintenance of the corporate form, than does operating as a corporation. Having said this, it is always advisable, from a best practices standpoint, to attempt "maintenance of the corporate form" in general by respecting the difference between the individual and the corporation or LLC.

If you incorporate as a subchapter C or S corporation, from the date of inception and filing of the Articles of Incorporation, the shareholders should always:

1. Maintain a formal corporate record book;
2. Schedule and conduct, after notice, regular and special meetings of the shareholders/officers/directors of the corporation;
3. Schedule and conduct, after notice, annual meetings of the corporation;
4. Issue consent resolutions based on the vote of shareholders/officers/directors at any and all meetings held for a corporate purpose;
5. Generally document all major decisions of the corporation, and include and maintain these documents in the corporate record book ("going concern" and daily activities need not be documented).

If you organize as an LLC, rigorous maintenance of the corporate form is generally considered not to be required in order to gain the benefit of limited liability for the members, however the more attempts and activities that demonstrate the separation between members and the company, the better. In the event an attempt is made to "pierce the corporate veil" and thus reach the assets of a member of an LLC, the analysis that will be undertaken by a court in this regard will be a weighted analysis. The number of factors that support separation between members and an LLC, compared with the number of factors which support that the member and the LLC are one and the same.

Balancing of these factors will ultimately determine if limited liability will be maintained or denied, although again, generally speaking this analysis augers more favorably toward the maintenance of limited liability when considered in connection with LLCs.

The Assumed Name

A very hyper-technical aspect of limited liability, as it pertains to the manner in which any LLC presents to the public, is the use of "assumed names" or DBAs ("doing business as").

An oftentimes overlooked concept among attorneys and laypeople alike, this is the improper use of a corporate name in commerce. Specifically, the use of the corporate entity name which is not reflected in the books and records of the state of Michigan, as incorporated or formed (LLC). In short, one should not, under any circumstances, present a corporate name to the public, either through signage, letterhead, or other publication, which is not exactly consistent with what name is filed in the Articles of Incorporation (corporation) or formation (LLC) with the state of Michigan.

For example, if your company is filed with the state as "Green Medical Marijuana and Sons, LLC", you should not maintain published notices to the public that read "GMM & Sons" or "Green Medical." Doing so potentially involves you operating as what is called an "undisclosed principal", potentially destroying all limited liability otherwise provided by forming the LLC. Such minor oversight can result in the complete eradication of limited liability.

This situation is easily remedied by filing an assumed name certificate with the state (LARA) in the event you wish to utilize a moniker with the public that does not utilize the "as filed" corporate name (often, principals do not wish to use/publish corporate designations with the public (Inc./LLC)).

Insuring that a corporation or LLC has properly filed an assumed name certificate with the state of Michigan, which accurately reflects the specific name being used in commerce with the public at large, cannot be over-emphasized, based on the potential for loss of limited liability such a failure could cause.

Employment Issues

This subsection is not intended to be exhaustive but it is important for all business owners to understand that employment issues in any business constitute a cottage industry within any one business. That is to say, regulating and managing company employees ends up consuming a great deal of corporate effort and management activities.

The key issues are the type of employees any one business may maintain. In short, the two key types of employees relating to closely held businesses are W-2 employees (tax withholding) or independent contractors. These are two very different categories. W-2 employees are those a company hires directly, and withholds payroll tax as required under federal and state law. Independent contractors actually are not employees at all, but contractors, independently hired as journeymen in effect.

The Sixth Circuit Court of Appeals in *Keller v. Miri Microsystems,* LLC, No. 14-1439 (6th Cir. 2015) clarified the distinction between an independent contractor and an employee under the Fair Labor Standards Act of 1938 (FLSA), 29 U.S.C. §207. The distinction is important as employees are entitled to certain benefits under the Fair Labor Standards Act (FLSA) (such as overtime pay), while independent contractors are not.

In Keller, a satellite dish installer agreed to work as an independent contractor to an installation company, but later filed a lawsuit against the company claiming he was an employee and entitled to overtime pay under the FLSA.

The court found that the fact that the worker was labeled as an independent contractor was not determinative, and remanded the case back to trial court to determine whether or not the worker should be treated as an employee and entitled to overtime benefits.

Upon remand, the trial court will apply the economic-reality test, which is the test to determine whether or not someone is an employee for purposes of the FLSA. There are six factors that are considered and weighed under the economic-reality test:

- The permanency of the relationship between the parties. Generally, a more permanent relationship weighs in favor of a worker being an employee.
- How much skill is required to perform the job in question. Skill level is another indicator because situations in which a worker's profits increase based on initiative, judgment, or foresight tend to support a finding that the worker is an independent contractor.
- The worker's personal investment in equipment or materials for the job. Comparing the amount of capital put into a job by the worker and by the employer is also an indicator. If the worker has invested a significant amount of their own capital into equipment or tools for the job, they are likely to be considered an independent contractor. This usually does not include equipment necessary for the job that can also be used by the worker for unrelated purposes, such as a vehicle.
- The worker's opportunity for more or less profit depending upon their skill. The greater control a worker has over the profitability of their job, the more likely they are to be considered an independent contractor.
- The degree of the alleged employer's right to control the manner in which the work is performed. The greater control a worker has over their schedule and manner of performing work, the more likely they are an independent contractor.
- Whether the services in question are an integral part of the alleged employer's business. The more integral the worker's

services are to the business, the less likely they are an independent contractor under the FLSA. In addition, the court sometimes considers additional factors such as whether or not the business had authority to hire or fire the worker and whether or not the business maintains the worker's employment records.

It is important to know these factors because a business owner could violate FLSA regulations without knowing it and unexpectedly be liable for things such as overtime pay to workers they believed were independent contractors. It is also important for workers to know their rights under FLSA's broad definition of employee, which was meant to prevent unfair labor practices.

Summary

Forming a corporation or organizing a limited liability company must be seriously considered by any group of potential shareholders or members who are considering a medical marijuana venture. The costs associated with forming an entity and maintaining same are outweighed by the significant benefits of limited liability afforded shareholders and members as to their personal assets.

Having said this, as suggested, depending on the entity choice, different "best practices" will be dictated and required of the shareholders/members/officers in order to maintain the benefit granted of incorporating a company or forming an LLC.

Issues such as equipment depreciation, size of business, financing and other issues will ramify on whether any one group of shareholders/members determines if a corporation or LLC is the proper entity choice. Almost invariably, it is worthwhile to consult with expert counsel (both general business and tax) to assist in making these critical decisions.

Once your business begins to grow, and the need to carry employees arises, engaging in best practices in this regard will go a long way to minimizing ongoing employee issues. Interaction with and management of corporate employees invariably becomes a cottage industry within any one company. Being aware of what type of employee is necessary, direct or independent contractor, and astutely managing your employees will always be critical to any business success.

In the end, the decision to elect to operate as a corporate entity is not one of "if", but of "which", in light of all the accrued benefits which result from incorporating a corporation or forming a limited liability company.

This Chapter Written By: Daniel J. McGlynn, J.D. / McGlynn Associates, P.L.L.C.

CHAPTER TWELVE

Intellectual Property

The Growing Need: Marijuana and Intellectual Property

It's clear that the marijuana industry is on the threshold of legitimization. This means that a significant amount of time, money, and energy will be spent on marketing, selling, and distributing marijuana products.

If a business can set aside all the discussions on the merits and dangers of ingestible, marijuana-based products, it will begin to see the powerful impact legalization is making on an industry that now must legitimize and safeguard its Intellectual Property (IP).

These facts are addressed in the article, "What a Looming Patent War Could Mean for the Future of the Marijuana Industry", by Greg Walters. The article referenced United States Patent No. 9,095,554, stating:

> On August 4, 2015, US officials quietly made history by approving the first-ever patent for a plant containing significant amounts of THC, the main psychoactive ingredient in marijuana, according to the patent's holders, their lawyers, and outside experts in intellectual property law.

More people are becoming aware that we are on the threshold of a brave new world, where legalized marijuana is going to drive great changes in the way consumers look at the now legitimate industry.

One marijuana grower noted that:

> "It's going to be a mess," said Tim Blake, a longtime grower and activist who founded California's annual Emerald Cup cannabis competition. "Marijuana growers developing new varieties are going to have to spend a lot of money on attorneys."

The reality is that just like any other business, anyone working in the marijuana industry will need to start protecting their assets, including their intellectual property. Whether a business is growing, supplying products to the industry, or distributing marijuana related products to consumers, IP is not only important, it is critical. Those who fail to secure their IP risk losing brand recognition, brand equity, and market share, while minimizing their business growth.

Every business has IP. If it is handled properly, it can be extremely valuable. Financial experts will typically place the value of a properly maintained and protected intellectual property portfolio at one-third the value of the business.

For example, the Kellogg Company acquired Keebler for an estimated $4.5 billion. A driving factor in that purchase price was the intellectual property portfolio which is represented by Ernie the Keebler Elf. At 1/3 the value of the business, financial experts would estimate the value of the intellectual property portfolio at around $1.5 billion.

It may be argued that one of the most important assets in that portfolio is this elf. He represents the brand and is the public persona for Keebler cookies. He is easily identifiable, just as identifiable as the Keebler name, another important intellectual property asset in the portfolio. That makes Ernie a very valuable elf. Every business has their own elf. Maybe not a $1.5 billion elf, but still a very valuable elf.

This brand recognition and value will fast become a critical factor for all businesses that decide to enter the multi-billion dollar marijuana industry. These businesses need to protect their IP elf.

Types of Intellectual Property

Leaders in the marijuana industry would be served well by taking crash courses in IP, and understanding the four types of intellectual property:

1. Trademarks
2. Patents
3. Copyrights
4. Trade Secrets

Let's take a moment to look at each one of these properties individually, and their potential impact on the marijuana industry.

Trademarks

Trademarks are synonymous with brands, a more commonly used term these days. A trademark is generally defined as, "a symbol, word, or words legally registered or established by use as representing a company or product." A service mark is the same except it represents a service, not a product. For purposes of this chapter, I will refer to both trademarks and service marks as trademarks, unless I need to make a specific point concerning service marks.

Trademark Protection for the Marijuana Industry

Trademarks are protected under common, state, and federal law. The most valuable trademark protection is federal trademark protection. There are a number of important benefits attached to owning a federal trademark registration. But, if a business product violates the Controlled Substances Act, a business is prohibited from obtaining federal trademark protection for the trademark associated with that product or service.

We conducted trademark research related to marijuana and cannabis in federal trademark applications. We performed a keyword search using the terms "cannabis" and "marijuana" to determine how many federal trademarks/trademark applications have been filed, issued, and abandoned.

- Cannabis (584) – Issued (96), Pending (194), Abandoned (294)
- Marijuana (292) – Issued (70), Pending (58), Abandoned (164)

The most prevalent goods and services associated with the "marijuana" and/or "cannabis" marks, in descending order, include:

1. Educational services (INT. CL. 41)
2. Clothing (INT. CL. 25)
3. Advertisement, marketing, and advocacy (INT. CL. 35)
4. Supplements (INT. CL. 5)

We compared the prosecution history, the official proceedings between the applicant and the USPTO, of registered trademarks and abandoned trademark applications. From our research, it appears that the overwhelming majority of abandoned trademark applications failed to respond to office actions with Section 2(e)(1) refusals (merely descriptive), and Sections 1 & 45 refusals (not in lawful use in commerce) or a request for the applicant to submit a written statement indicating whether the goods and/or services identified in the application comply with the Controlled Substances Act (CSA).

In order to overcome the Section 2(e)(1) refusals, some of the issued marks changed their classification of goods or services, or amended to the Supplemental Register. (See the mark "ONLINE MARIJUANA DESIGN" – reg.4872203).

While a few marks are able to provide additional information to overcome the Sections 1 & 45 refusals (See "MEDICAL MARIJUANA" – reg. 4024120), many trademark applications facing a Sections 1 & 45 refusal changed the mark and/or description of goods and services. (See "MARIJUANA PHARMACEUTICALS PHARMACEUTICAL GRADE MEDICAL MARIJUANA" – Reg. 4862260, which received a final office action before the mark was re-filed under a different class by the same owner).

When applying for US Federal Trademark protection, if the examiner suspects that the trademark involves marijuana, the following requirement is made of the applicant.

> In addition, applicant must submit a written statement indicating whether all the services identified in the application comply with relevant federal law, including the Controlled Substances Act (CSA), 21 U.S.C. §§801-971. See 37 C.F.R. §2.69; TMEP §907. The CSA prohibits, among other things, manufacturing, distributing, dispensing, or possessing certain controlled substances, including marijuana and marijuana-based preparations. 21 U.S.C. §§812, 841(a)(1), 844(a); see also 21 U.S.C. §802(16) (defining "[marijuana]"). The CSA also makes it unlawful to sell, offer for sale, or use any facility of interstate commerce to transport drug paraphernalia, i.e., "any equipment, product, or material of any kind which is primarily intended or designed for use in manufacturing, compounding, converting, concealing, producing, processing, preparing, injecting, ingesting, inhaling, or otherwise introducing into the human body a controlled substance, possession of which is unlawful under [the CSA]." 21 U.S.C. §863.
>
> Finally, the applicant must provide written responses to the following questions:
>
> - "Do applicant's identified services involve the sale, provision, and/or possession of marijuana, marijuana-based preparations, or marijuana extracts or derivatives, synthetic marijuana, or any other illegal controlled substances?"
>
> - "Are the applicant's services lawful pursuant to the Controlled Substances Act?"
>
> Failure to satisfactorily respond to a requirement for information is a ground for refusing registration. See In re Cheezwhse.com, Inc., 85 USPQ2d 1917, 1919 (TTAB 2008); In re Garden of Eatin' Inc., 216 USPQ 355, 357 (TTAB 1982); TMEP §814. Please note that merely stating that information about the services is available on applicant's website is an inappropriate response to the above requirement and is insufficient to make the relevant information properly of record. See In re Planalytics, Inc., 70 USPQ2d 1453, 1457-58 (TTAB 2004).

This requirement is a major obstacle to the registration of trademarks related to the marijuana business. This poses a major concern since trademarks and more importantly federally registered trademarks are extremely valuable business assets. This requirement is not likely to go away any time soon. Even though marijuana businesses face this obstacle, it doesn't diminish the need to still select good brands and protect a business's trademarks.

So how are marijuana related businesses getting Federal Trademark Registrations? They appear to be re-characterizing (mischaracterizing) their businesses. For example, a resale store becomes an advertising service for marijuana products. Whether these new characterizations will hold up to legal challenges is yet to be decided. But, since these issues will be decided by federal courts, the likely result may be a loss of these mischaracterized trademarks.

Trademarks Available for the Marijuana Industry

In the United States, trademarks are obtained through use. Under common law, once a mark has been used and is capable of distinguishing a source for goods or services, it is a trademark and has common law trademark rights.

Generally speaking, these rights are limited to the geographic area in which the mark is used, which could be local, statewide, regional etc. Although valuable, they lack the substantial benefits of state and federal registration.

State trademark registration is the next level of protection for trademarks. Michigan has a state trademark registration law. It is officially the Trademarks and Service Marks Act of 1960 P.A. 242, and is modeled after the federal law governing trademarks (The Lanham Act). The Michigan Act defines a trademark as:

> Any word, name, symbol, or device, or any combination thereof, other than a trade name in its entirety, adopted and used by a person to identify goods made or sold by him or her and to distinguish them from similar goods made or sold by others.

State trademark registration only extends to use within the state. In Michigan, there is no direct prohibition in the statute against registration of marks related to the marijuana business. The statue prohibits the registration of a trademark that consists of or comprises immoral, deceptive, or scandalous matter (see 429.32(a)). None of these would appear to be a reason for refusing registration of trademarks related to legal marijuana related businesses, such as medical marijuana related trademarks.

Things to Remember About Trademarks

It's important to note that many businesses make the mistake of thinking that registration of a trade name in Michigan gives them the right to that name as a trademark. As clearly indicated in the Michigan Act, trade names are specifically excluded. Registering a state trademark is a more involved process wherein the state refuses to allow confusingly similar trademarks to be registered. In contrast, trade name registration just requires that the names be different, a much less demanding process. Also, registration of either a trademark or trade name does not confer the right to use a mark. Others may have superior rights by having used the mark previously.

The only way to determine whether a business is free to use a mark as a trademark is to have a search done to locate any other confusingly similar uses. This will be discussed further below.

The best form of trademark protection is federal registration; although presently unavailable for many in the marijuana business. A trademark is eligible for federal registration if the mark is used in interstate commerce. Interstate commerce is generally defined as commerce between the states. Therefore, a mark used in more than one state is eligible for federal registration. Federal registration of a trademark is obtained by filing an application for registration with the United States Patent and Trademark Office. The United States Trademark Office examines the application. If it meets all of the requirements, it is registered. The registration is good for an initial five years and then additional 10-year periods thereafter upon the filing of renewal requests.

A trademark application is examined to determine whether it is confusingly similar to any other registered trademarks. It is the duty of the examiner to refuse to register confusingly similar trademarks.

This is an important point for trademark owners to consider. It is not advisable to select a trademark that is confusingly similar to the trademarks of others since such a mark will be difficult to register and enforce.

To determine whether they are confusingly similar, the examiner and the courts look at the similarity between 1) the marks and 2) the goods or services. The general test applied by the courts is whether the consumer will be confused. It is acceptable to have a trademark that is the same, similar or closely related to another's trademark if the goods and services are sufficiently different so that the consuming public will not be confused.

For example, most people recognize Apple as the company making and selling computers, phones, etc. and in the music business, i.e. iTunes. Some music lovers will also recognize Apple in connection with Apple Records. Both of these marks existed for many years without any problems because their goods and services did not overlap. In the beginning, Apple was involved with computers and Apple Records was in the music business. They could exist without issue. When Apple moved into the music business, iTunes, there was an overlap and subsequent litigation between the two parties that continued for decades.

Continuing with this example, some student drivers will recognize Apple in connection with Apple driving schools, again no overlap and no problem. Lastly by way of example there is Apple used in connection with promotional services for student athletes that is a registered trademark. Because there is no overlap in goods and services, there is no problem.

There are numerous advantages to federal registration. Of particular importance is that it confers upon the registrant constructive use throughout the United States. Instead of being limited to the geographic area of use under common law or the state under state trademark registration, use is conferred throughout the United States. After five years the mark can become incontestable which provides advantages in protecting the mark from use by others and in litigation proceedings. Basically, incontestability shields the mark against challenges to invalidity of the mark based upon descriptiveness. Federal registration allows the use of ® to identify the mark as a registered mark. The federal courts have jurisdiction over disputes involving federal registered trademarks. The mark is easy to find when others are considering choosing a mark. The first place most researchers review is the federal register which is publicly available and if a business' mark is registered, most sophisticated businesses will not choose that mark. There are additional advantages, but for purposes of this chapter, these are the most important.

Choosing a Trademark

When choosing a mark, it is important to select a mark that is strong and not confusingly similar to other trademarks. The chart below shows the relative strength of marks, from generic, which have no strength and cannot act as trademarks, to the strongest, fanciful, or coined trademarks. The stronger the trademark the easier it is to protect. It is difficult to argue that a business decision to select the same coined or fanciful trademark was inadvertent, or that it won't confuse consumers.

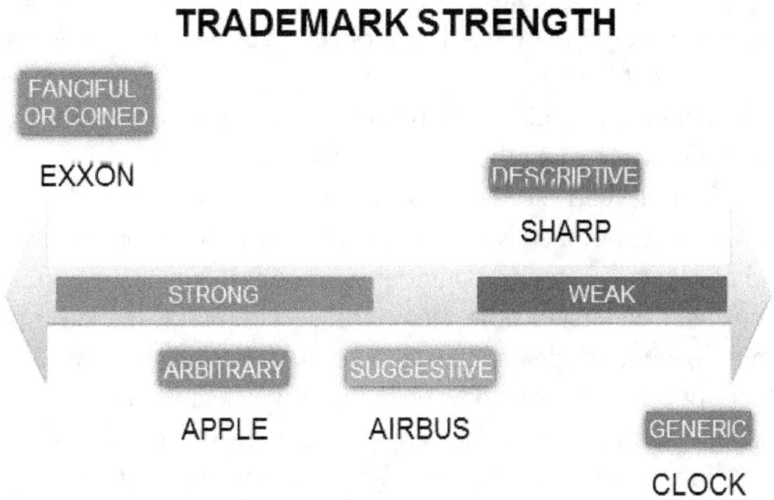

Trademarks are one of a business' most valuable assets. It is the brand. It is how customers will find them and remember everything about them. It symbolizes everything that is great about a business. The trademark should grow in value as a business grows. It provides flexibility on how a business grows, a strong, well-recognized trademark can open the door to later licensing opportunities, product expansion, and franchising capabilities. Companies need to carefully choose this valuable asset.

Two Questions to Answer

There are two questions to answer when choosing a trademark or brand. First, can it be protected, and second, is it clear? To be protected a mark must be as strong as possible so that it can keep competitors from adopting similar trademarks that confuse customers.

To say it differently, if the mark is weak others could adopt a mark that is close to the one selected and ride on the business' success. If the business is successful, others will want to take unfair advantage of that success. They will want to adopt trademarks that are close to the successful business so that they can confuse consumers into believing that they are somehow associated with those popular products. This can result in numerous problems for a business including lost sales, lower profits, and damaged reputation due to the actions of others. The stronger a business mark, the easier it is to protect.

A trademark is clear when a business is free to use the mark without concern that others will challenge its use, i.e. sue the business. Getting sued is a scenario all businesses should avoid.

The best approach is to pick a number of options for trademarks and have them reviewed by trademark counsel. He or she can help a business understand the weak and strong marks and do a preliminary low-cost clearance search to uncover any clear problems. Once the list is narrowed, a business may select its best choice(s) and have it fully searched for any possible clearance issues.

A full search should then be done to uncover not only registered trademarks but also common law trademarks. Full searches are very complete comprehensive searches. IP counsel will then review the search results and render an opinion as to both strength and availability. Only then can a business be confident in its trademark and grow its brand within its business.

Patents

In its broadest sense, patents protect inventions. In the United States a patent is granted to an inventor by the United States Patent Office. A patent gives the owner the right to exclude others from making, using, selling, or importing an invention throughout the United States. The owner may license or sell the rights. Without a patent, anyone can make and sell an invention without permission and without compensation.

The United States Patent Laws are codified in US Code: Title 35 – Patents.

35 USC § 101 defines what inventions can be patented:

> Whoever invents or discovers any new and useful process, machine, manufacture, or composition of matter, or any new and useful improvement thereof, may obtain a patent therefor, subject to the conditions and requirements of this title.

Plant Patents

35 USC § 161 defines what plants can be patented:

> Whoever invents or discovers and asexually reproduces any distinct and new variety of plant, including cultivated sports, mutants, hybrids, and newly found seedlings, other than a tuber propagated plant or a plant found in an uncultivated state, may obtain a patent therefor, subject to the conditions and requirements of this title.

Patents are important to businesses. Any business that invents or that is involved in the production of asexually reproduced plants should consider patent protection. This includes the marijuana business.

The United States Patent and Trademark Office (USPTO) does not appear to be concerned that marijuana and marijuana related technology violates federal law. The USPTO has issued numerous patents on marijuana related technology and on methods of using marijuana for specific medical treatments. In fact, the United States government has its own United States patent, US patent number 6,630,507, for a method of using certain cannabinoids for specific medical treatment.

As reported by George Anders in his article, "Marijuana's Patent Spree Puts The 'High' In High Tech":

> Some 266 marijuana-related patents have been approved in the U.S., and another 255 are pending, according to a new analysis by Envision IP, a Raleigh, N.C., patent-research firm. These filings cover everything from proprietary hybrid strains of cannabis, to "clean and efficient growing systems, software-based analytics and monitoring, and packaging and distribution infrastructure..."
>
> By Envision IP's tally, nearly 20 companies now hold cannabis-related patents. Among the most active are AbbVie, Jenrin Discovery and Cara Therapeutics.

Quartz Media reported in its article titled, "The US Government Grants Cannabis Patents Even Though Weed is Illegal", Teewinot Life Sciences reported the issuance of United States Patent No. 9,587,213 for its apparatus and methods for biosynthetic production of cannabinoids. The article also reports that Patent No. 9,095,554, was granted in August 2015 to a group of California weed growers. This was the first patent for a plant strain containing "significant amounts" of THC.

Another good article relating to the importance of patents to the marijuana industry is, "Want Your Marijuana Start Up to Succeed?", Study Patent Law.

Getting Patent Protection for Your Invention

The United States Patent and Trademark Office (the USPTO) grants patents. A carefully drafted patent application is required. This is not an ordinary "fill in the blank application", it is a document that must be created by a skilled practitioner. There are numerous rules and regulations that must be complied with to obtain patent protection. Once the application is complete, it is filed with the USPTO. A patent examiner then examines the application for form, substance, and ultimately patentability.

Once examined and if patentable, the application can issue. A utility patent is valid from 20 years from its earliest filing or priority date as long as the required maintenance fees are paid at 3½, 7½ and 11½ years. Design patents are valid for 15 years from the date of grant. Plant patents are valid for 20 years from their earliest filing or priority date with no requirement to pay maintenance fees.

Foreign patents are also available and can be based upon a business' US patent application.

Copyright

Federal registration of copyrights provides valuable benefits, is relatively easy to obtain, and is inexpensive. Copyrights protect many things that are common to businesses such as brochures, proposals, sales materials, websites, photos of products, webinars, white papers, computer software, architectural plans, and more.

In the broadest sense, copyrights protect original works of authorship fixed in any tangible medium of expression. Copyrights are obtained immediately upon fixing a work of authorship in tangible form. Copyright registration provides additional benefits. However, registration is not required to have copyright protection.

In the business context, works of authorship typically include written works such as books, pamphlets, advertising materials, photographs, artwork, videos, webinars, computer software, architecture, etc.

17 USC § 106 of The Copyright Act generally gives the owner of copyright a bundle of rights including the exclusive right to reproduce the work in copies, prepare derivative works based upon the work, distribute copies of the work to the public by sale or other transfer of ownership, or by rental, lease, or lending, or to perform the work publicly, in the case of audio visual works and sound recordings (see 17 USC § 106).

Copyrights last a long time. Copyright in a work created on or after January 1, 1978, subsists from its creation and, except as provided by the following exceptions, endures for a term consisting of the life of the author and 70 years after the author's death. If it is a joint work, prepared by two or more authors who did not work for hire, the copyright endures for a term consisting of the life of the last surviving author and 70 years after such last surviving author's death. In the case of an anonymous work, a pseudonymous work, or a work made for hire, the copyright endures for a term of 95 years from the year of its first publication, or a term of 120 years from the year of its creation, whichever expires first.

If a copyright is infringed, the infringer of copyright is liable for either the copyright owner's actual damages and any additional profits of the infringer, or statutory damages. The court is also authorized to grant an injunction against further infringement (17 USC § 504).

The copyright owner may elect an award of statutory damages for all infringements involved in the action, with respect to any one work, in a sum of not less than $750 or more than $30,000 as the court considers just. In a case where the infringement was committed willfully, the court in its discretion may increase the award of statutory damages to a sum of not more than $150,000. But, statutory damages are only available in the United States for works that were registered with the Copyright Office prior to infringement, or within three months of publication (17 U.S.C. § 412).

Obviously, if the material is important to a business, it should be registered.

WARNING: Who Owns the Copyright

Even though copyrights are relatively easy to obtain, businesses make a common mistake with regard to ownership. Copyrights are initially owned by the author and that ownership transfers only through a written document or through a legal theory known as "work for hire." The United States Supreme Court in the case of *Community for Creative Nonviolence v. Reid*, 490 US 730 (1989) interpreted the copyright statute and in particular ownership. The Supreme Court case involved a sculpture depicting the plight of the homeless created by the sculptor Reid. The Community for Creative Nonviolence retained Reid to create the sculpture. The sculpture depicted a family in Washington DC living on a street grate.

The Center for Creative Nonviolence decided to take the sculpture on the road to generate support for their cause. Reid objected to the plan, arguing that he had the right under copyright law to control display of the work. The issue before the Supreme Court was who owned the copyright and therefore the right to display the sculpture. The Center for Creative Nonviolence argued that they owned the copyright because it was a work for hire. They argued that they paid Reid to sculpt the work and that they should own all rights to the work.

The Supreme Court of the United States held that to be a work for hire, the author had to be an employee under the common definition of an employee. Basically, the employee couldn't be an independent contractor, but had to be a true employee. The Supreme Court held that Reid was an independent contractor and as such owned the work. Since the work was not a work for hire, the only way to transfer ownership of the copyright was through a written agreement assigning copyright.

The take away for a business is the need to have a written agreement that assigns the work to the business and in the alternative that the work is a work for hire.

The likelihood of ownership of copyright arising in business is more common than expected. Many businesses utilize third parties to develop various marketing materials, including websites, sales materials like brochures, and more. The business should own the copyrights since they are paying the third parties to develop the copyrighted material. To ensure the business owns the copyright, an agreement needs to be reached with any third parties ensuring that the copyrights are assigned to the business or in some very narrow circumstances establishing that the work is a work made for hire. Since the typical situation is the business hiring of a third party, a written agreement assigning those works to the business is needed.

An agreement is also advisable with employees as well. If the person is an employee, and the person is hired to develop certain intellectual property, then it is a work for hire since it is within the employee's job description. The issue becomes when an employee is assigned a task that is not within their job description. In those instances, the written agreement assigning the intellectual property to the business is needed. To make sure the business owns its employees' copyrightable creations, their employment agreements should have provisions assigning such rights to the business.

Getting Copyright Protection

The United States Copyright Office grants copyrights. It requires an application for registration and the submission of samples of the work. The application is examined for formalities and the registration is granted. The Copyright Office provides the necessary forms online. Copyright registration is relatively easy and inexpensive. Copyright registrations should be a regular addition to a well-managed intellectual property portfolio.

Trade Secrets

Trade secrets protect anything the business considers to be a secret. This can include customer information, supplier information, systems used in the business, formulas, recipes, top selling products, future plans of the business, expansion plans, etc. The typical way of protecting trade secrets is through an agreement with any party that has access to the business' secrets to keep them a secret. In order to remain a trade secret, it must be a secret maintained by the business.

Until May 11, 2016, theft of trade secret cases were only brought in state courts and that state's trade secret laws typically applied.

There is now federal jurisdiction for trade secret theft. The Defend Trade Secrets Act of 2016 (DTSA) was signed into law on May 11, 2016. The DTSA's purpose is to create a national law instead of the various state trade secret laws. Cases are brought in federal courts. It is intended to provide more certainty for litigants in trade secrets cases.

In addition to enjoining the use of misappropriated trade secrets, the DTSA contains a seizure provision that allows for the seizure of stolen trade secrets in "extraordinary circumstances." This is done through an "ex parte application," meaning the trade secret owner can request the order without the accused party being present. The requirements for such an order are set forth in the DTSA and require a number of factors to be proven.

A common way that trade secrets are misappropriated is when an employee leaves the business and uses the information to his or her advantage in a new business or for a new employer. Businesses should have agreements with their employees, particularly key employees, regarding trade secrets and the need for confidentiality. These agreements are extremely helpful in the event that trade secrets are misappropriated. Many times, providing the new employer and former employee with a copy of the agreement can lead to an amicable resolution of the issue. If litigation is required, agreements can be helpful in establishing the existence of trade secrets and the employee's knowledge of them. Trade secret agreements are also important with respect to third parties who have or may come into contact with a business' trade secret information. They should be used with investors, suppliers, consultants, joint development partners, etc. Anyone that may come into contact with secret information should have a trade secret agreement.

In preparing these agreements, it is important to keep in mind that the DTSA has an immunity provision for whistleblowers. The immunity provision generally provides that a person cannot be held criminally or civilly liable for revealing trade secrets to a federal, state, or local government official, or to an attorney. The DTSA requires that employers provide notice of this immunity in any contract or agreement with an employee that governs the use of trade secrets or other confidential information. If the employer fails to do this, the employer cannot be awarded exemplary damages or attorneys' fees in an action against an employee to whom notice was not provided.

Avoiding Litigation

Avoiding intellectual property litigation should be as important to a business as acquiring intellectual property assets. Intellectual property litigation can be avoided as long as a business recognizes the intellectual property of competitors and protects a business from that intellectual property.

Copyright litigation is easy to avoid, just don't copy. Trademark litigation is also fairly easy to avoid, as discussed above, be careful in the selection of a business' trademarks. Don't pick marks that can lead to litigation. Trade secrets are mainly avoided by care in business hiring processes. If a business is hiring an employee from a competitor, be careful to discuss trade secrets with the new employee and have him or her understand the consequences of bringing secrets from the former employer. It would be advisable to have a policy statement regarding the use of information from former employers in a business, so that a business can discuss that policy with any new employees.

Patent litigation is a different beast. Every new product launch creates the potential for patent litigation. Patent clearance searches and opinions must be done to ensure a business is not violating the patent rights of others. Any time a business is launching a new product, the business must recognize that there could be issues, and plan on meeting with counsel to review those issues and make sure that the business is protected against any infringement problems. A business can infringe a patent and not be aware that the patent exists until receiving a threatening letter from the patent owner.

To find potential problem patents, a search needs to be conducted. Normally, an initial search of a business competitors' patents is done to locate potential issues. If a business is fortunate, it may also find patent numbers on related products. Researchers then use various search strategies and methods to complete the search.

Once all relevant patents have been located, an opinion is rendered as to the scope of potential patent issues. If a potential problem is discovered, the claims must be reviewed to determine whether there would be infringement issues and if they can be avoided or designed around. Lastly, if infringement cannot be avoided, then the patents must be reviewed for validity. Although patents are presumed valid, they can be invalidated, i.e. rendered useless, by several legal defenses.

An example of a product that ultimately avoided patent infringement is shown below. This is an example of designing around a patent to avoid infringement. These are guide rails for retractable rubber doors. They keep the door in the track but allow the door to be released upon impact.

The patent covered the product on the left. The company knew of the patent on the product and thought that it covered an extruded aluminum rail. An extruded aluminum rail was described in the patent description, but was not actually claimed. The company, without the advice of counsel, decided that if they used plastic inserts they would not infringe the patent.

They launched their product and were sued for patent infringement. The patent actually covered the profile of the fingers closing the opening. See the arrow in the first figure. The company was advised to use a square insert as shown on the far right. The square design does not infringe the claims. This design change ultimately resulted in settlement of the lawsuit. This was a fairly simple design around to end an expensive lawsuit.

An example of invalidating a patent to avoid patent infringement is the Keebler elves fight over the Chips Ahoy packaging.

An investigation uncovered that the package was disclosed in a publication that was published more than a year before the chip's patent was filed which invalidated their patent. A business can refer to the article for a more detailed explanation of the litigation, "How the Keebler Elves Fought Off Patent Infringement".

Case Study: Trynex

Two entrepreneurial brothers had the idea of making a better salt spreader. It was the classic beginning to a business. The brothers recognized a problem with traditional salt spreaders and decided they could make a better one. They then built a business around that idea.

The brothers started in the lawn and garden business mowing grass, plowing snow, and spreading salt with traditional salt spreaders. They were very successful in this business and parlayed that business into owning a retail lawn and garden business.

Through their use and sale of salt spreaders, they identified problems that they felt they could solve. One of their first challenges was to pick a name for their business. Initially, they wanted to name their business after a salt spreader product that they had successfully sold in the United States. Through their marketing savvy the product became very well-known and was a top seller.

The problem they faced was that another company owned the product name and adopting it would have likely created immediate litigation issues for the fledgling company.

Their IP counsel encouraged them to pick a different trademark and not spend money on litigation. They could invest the money they would have spent on litigation in getting their new name recognized. They chose a very strong trademark, Trynex. It is a coined trademark, one that is entirely made up, the strongest trademark one can have. They then created sub trademarks for products including SnowEx for salt spreaders.

Trynex is the good example of a business that handled their IP perfectly. From the beginning, the brothers were very interested in protecting all of their intellectual property, their trademarks, patents, copyrights and trade secrets. They were successful in obtaining strong trademark registration for their trademarks as well as patents on their innovations.

As the business grew, their registered trademarks, their brand, represented all their business success: customer service, distribution channels, quality products, and innovative ideas. They had several patents protecting their innovations allowing them to gain market share, and obtain higher margins on products. They had their marketing materials, white papers, published articles, all protected by copyrights. They were also very diligent in protecting their trade secrets.

So How Did They Do It?

They had a system to recognize, collect and protect their intellectual property. They met quarterly with IP counsel to review all of their new developments, to both add more to their intellectual property portfolio and to ensure that they steered clear of any litigation relating to the intellectual property of others. Together, we developed a three-step process, represented below by the symbols for trademarks, copyrights, and patents. The process involved ®ecognizing the potential for protectable intellectual property. The simple mantra we developed for recognizing intellectual property was: if it is important to the business, and the business doesn't want its competitors to have it, consider protecting it. They ©ollected the information through various systems and then we met once a quarter to discuss ℗rotecting the intellectual property that was recognized and collected. The key to their IP success was the process. We met quarterly without fail and reviewed everything that related to improving their IP portfolio.

®ECOGNIZE
©OLLECT
℗ROTECT

A few years ago, Trynex came to the attention of a major snowplow manufacturer who wanted to enter into the salt spreader business. It was publicly reported that they paid close to $30 million for Trynex. Experts would place the value of the intellectual property portfolio at close to $10 million.

It may be argued that the value was more, since the purchaser had the ability to enter the salt spreader business with little effort. In my opinion, the strong Trynex brand, their trademarks, and their patent protection added considerable value to the purchase price.

Summary

The marijuana industry needs to recognize the importance of IP in every aspect of their business.

It's imperative that intellectual property is recognized, collected, and protected. Intellectual property can protect markets, margins, pricing of products and services, and increase the overall asset value of the business.

What's more, marijuana professionals need to recognize the intellectual property held by others. Intellectual property litigation is expensive and distracting to a business, so it's better to tune in to what the competitors are protecting, in order to avoid expensive intellectual property litigation.

Leaders in the marijuana industry need to start thinking about how they will RECOGNIZE, COLLECT, and PROTECT their current and future IP.

Ultimately, the time has come for the marijuana industry to enter the world of mainstream business. This starts with the realization that every business has intellectual property, and that a legitimate business must care for its IP, while recognizing the intellectual property of others.

Anyone dealing in the legal marijuana industry would be wise to seek professional IP counsel on their current and future intellectual properties.

This Chapter Written By: William Honaker, J.D./Dickinson Wright, P.L.L.C.

CHAPTER THIRTEEN

Financing and Insuring Your Medical Marijuana Business

As with any business, medical marijuana businesses require financing, insurance, and tax planning. This chapter addresses two things in two separate parts. Part A primarily addresses the types of insurance you are either required by law to have, or that you should have to properly mitigate the risks specific to medical marijuana. The various accounting aspects of a medical marijuana business are addressed in Part B of this chapter. As with the other chapters in this book, neither part of this chapter is a substitute for the necessary legal, financial, or tax advice you will receive from a professional. Instead, this chapter will arm you with the basic information necessary to most efficiently utilize the related professional services.

PART A
Insuring Your Medical Marijuana Business

Like any other commercial enterprise, a medical marijuana business needs insurance to protect it from the risks associated with running that business. Many of the coverages will be familiar (e.g., worker's compensation, property, liability), while others are specific to the particulars of the business in question (e.g., crop insurance).

Of critical importance is the need for product liability insurance *prior* to applying for *any* MMMA license (MCL Sec. 4209.408(1)). Savvy business owners will recognize, however, that there are many other hazards associated with a medical marijuana business beyond the potential for bodily harm caused by adulterated product. The following is a summary of insurance issues faced by such businesses.

Insurance Common to All Licenses

1. **General Liability:** Insures against bodily injury and/or property damage caused by your business, your product, or your employee. This type of policy may include the product liability coverage required under the statute, or may exclude product liability in expectation that such coverage will be purchased separately on a stand-alone basis.

2. **Property:** Insures against damage to the building, contents, and other property of the business. Equipment breakdown covers sudden and accidental failures of machinery used in the business, and is where coverage for spoilage will be, if it is provided at all. Business interruption is a component of property insurance that kicks in following a covered loss to provide net income and certain normal operating expenses that continue during the restoration period.

3. **Worker's Compensation:** All Michigan businesses with employees must have worker's compensation insurance, which provides wage loss and medical expense indemnity for injured employees. Officers of a company operating without worker's compensation can be personally liable for any injury to an employee.

4. **Automobile:** Even businesses that do not own or use an automobile in their business need non-owned and hired auto

insurance, which protects the business for its vicarious liability arising from an employee using their personal car for company business. Examples are driving to meet with suppliers, advisors, or even driving to the post office. The auto exposure for businesses that own or lease cars or trucks obviously will be more involved.

5. **Management Liability**

    - *Director's and Officer's Liability (D&O):* Protects the business and its employees against claims of business torts (e.g., breach of contract) and may provide protection from regulators.
    - *Employment Practices Liability:* Protects against claims by employees of harassment and discrimination.
    - *Cyber Coverage:* The MMMA and its sister Marihuana Tracking Act require licensees to collect and maintain personal information of patients or other counterparties. Should your database containing this private information be compromised (by outside hackers or a disgruntled employee) Michigan privacy law imposes many expensive burdens on the database owner.

License-Specific Insurance Needs

1. Grower License (Class A, B, or C)

    - *Crop Insurance:* In addition to insuring the building, equipment, and tools needed to grow marijuana, addressed above, growers will need specific insurance to handle the plant during its three distinct stages:
        - Living plant material (e.g., seeds, seedlings, and plants still in the growth medium (mature or not).
        - Harvested plant material (e.g., plants and material removed from the growing medium for drying and curing).

  - Finished stock (plant material ready-for-sale).
  - Standard property policies will not cover damage to a grower's crop.
- *Pollution Insurance:* Most agribusinesses use chemicals and fertilizers, generate waste and wastewater, or otherwise have exposure to a release of potentially harmful contaminants.

2. Processor License
3. Provisioning Center (aka Dispensary)
4. Secure Transporter
5. Safety Compliance Facility

This Section Written By: Mark Fisher, J.D.

PART B
Assuring the Tax Compliance of Your Medical Marijuana Business

Overview

The one thing that is clear when it comes to determining taxable income is that income from the sale of marijuana is included. What is less clear is how you determine that income. From an accounting standpoint, sales minus cost of goods sold and operating expenses equals net income. For the sale of any controlled substance, however, you must look at Internal Revenue Code Section 280E which states, "no deduction or credit shall be allowed for any amount paid or incurred during the taxable year in carrying on any trade or business if such trade or business (or the activities which comprise such trade or business) consists of trafficking in controlled substances (within the meaning of Schedule I and II of the Controlled Substances Act) which is prohibited by Federal law or the law of any State in which such trade or business is conducted."

This means you are not allowed to deduct your operating expenses. However, case law has established a precedent to allow taxation of gross income and not gross receipts (Doyle V. Mitchell Bros. Co. 247 U.S. 179). The Internal Revenue Service (IRS) reached the conclusion that, "a taxpayer trafficking in a Schedule I or Schedule II controlled substance determines cost of goods sold using the applicable inventory-costing regulations under Internal Revenue Code Section 71 as they existed when Internal Revenue Code Section 280E was enacted." Thus, in determining gross receipts you are allowed to deduct cost of goods sold.

Determining Cost of Goods Sold

With the issuance of CCA20150411 by the IRS on January 23, 2015, the IRS provided guidance that the "Full-Absorption" method may be used to account for cost of goods sold and inventory. Under Full-Absorption accounting, a grower can account for all expenses incurred in growing product as either an expense or part of inventory for any unsold product at year-end. Thus, the following expenses when incurred in a growing operation can be partially or fully tax deductible:

- Rent
- Utilities
- Supplies (i.e., soil, nutrients)
- Seeds
- Tools and equipment
- Labor
- Real estate and personal property taxes
- Repairs and maintenance to growing equipment
- Any other costs related to production

Many expenses, including, but not limited to, rent, utilities, and labor, may need to be allocated between production and non-production. For example, if you rent a facility and ninety percent of the facility is used for growing and production and ten percent for administrative offices, then ten percent of the rent would be a general and administrative expense and not deductible.

In addition, you must allocate the deductible expense between goods sold during the year and inventory at the end of the year. For example, if you cultivate three crops during the year and your fourth crop is fully grown but not sold, you would allocate seventy-five percent of your production costs to what has been sold. The remaining twenty-five percent of production costs would be allocated to inventory and deducted in the following year when the inventory is sold.

For dispensaries, unless there is another business being run at the same facility as the dispensary, the dispensary can only deduct the cost of product that is sold. If more than one business is being run out of the same facility, a reasonable allocation of expenses must be made between the various businesses. The portion of expenses (rent, utilities, insurance, etc.) allocable to the other businesses operated at the facility would be deductible. (*Champs v. Commissioner*, 128 T.C. 173 (2007) set the precedent to allow for an allocation of expenses between two or more trades or businesses).

Cash Reportable Transactions

Each person engaged in a trade or business who, in the course of that trade or business, receives more than $10,000 in cash in one transaction or in two or more related transactions must file Form 8300 - Report of Cash Payments Over $10,000 Received in a Trade or Business with the Internal Revenue Service and keep a copy of the filing for five years. You must disclose the identity and taxpayer identification number of the person who made the payment(s) when completing Form 8300. Willful failure to file a correct and complete Form 8300 can be subject to a minimum penalty of $25,000.

Michigan Tax Considerations

Individual income taxes start with federal adjusted gross income. Thus, the rules previously discussed regarding deductible expenses apply in determining taxable income for Michigan.

Michigan also imposes a three percent excise tax on the gross retail income of a licensed medical marijuana provisioning center. In addition, the sale of medical marijuana in Michigan is subject to the state's six percent sales tax. The retail seller is responsible for the collection and remittance of the sales tax to the Michigan Department of Treasury.

Complete Accounting

Under regulation 1.446-1(a)(4), the IRS requires taxpayers to maintain accounting records that will allow the taxpayer to file a correct tax return for each tax period. This means that you should have invoices for each sale and receipts to document each purchase and expense item. Without proper records and documentation, in the event of an audit, an expense may be disallowed since the burden of proof falls upon the taxpayer.

Consult a Tax Advisor

Due to the complex nature of the federal tax laws regarding what expenses are deductible in a business that grows marijuana or sells marijuana at retail, as well as the related state tax laws, it is strongly recommended that you engage an experienced tax advisor to assist you in adhering to the tax rules and compliance requirements.

This Section Written By: Jeff Ellis, C.P.A. / Edwards, Ellis, Stanley, Armstrong, Bowren, Krizan & Company, P.C.

Conclusion

We hope that you enjoyed this book about medical marijuana business licensing. Undoubtedly you learned a lot, and perhaps even decided that the medical marijuana industry is not for you. On the other hand, you may now be more excited than ever. Either way, thank you for taking the time to buy and read this important resource.

We also expect that this book answered many of your questions regarding getting licensed and starting a medical marijuana business. But, this book probably did not answer every conceivable question that you have. This is because you might have questions regarding your specific situation that could not be covered in this general overview. If you have additional questions, feel free to contact my office. We are happy to answer the remaining questions that you have.

Additionally, if you are ready to apply for licensing but you need assistance with the process, contact the Barone Defense Firm. We can make this process easier for you by filling out paperwork, gathering necessary documents, and making sure that everything is done right the first time. In the long run, making sure that everything is correct the first time is going to save you time and money.

If you would like to set up a consultation with the Barone Defense Firm, then please contact us at 248-594-4554. You can also visit one of our offices for more information. Our locations are:

280 N Old Woodward Avenue #200
Birmingham, MI 48009

61 Commerce Avenue SW #504
Grand Rapids, MI 49503

All the authors are available for consultation, and will welcome your call. Contact Dan McGlynn with your business formation questions, Bill Honaker regarding your intellectual property concerns, Jeff Ellis for accounting and Mark Fisher regarding insurance and financing. Their biographical information is listed in the authors section. Please visit their websites to learn more about their services and to obtain specific contact information.

Finally, please know that collectively, we took the time to write this book because we love helping people like you. This is why we look forward to taking your call and learning more about you. We also look forward to having the privilege of working with you as you embark on an exciting new chapter in your life!

About the Author and Contributors

Patrick T. Barone

Patrick T. Barone began his legal career in 1988 when he was a Judicial Law Clerk to the Honorable Richard D. Kuhn of the Oakland County Circuit Court. In 1992, he opened his law practice and initially he handled hundreds of disparate felony criminal matters in the adult and juvenile courts. In 1999, Patrick decided to focus exclusively on cases involving allegations of intoxicated driving. Almost immediately thereafter, Patrick quickly began to establish a national reputation for being among the best DUI defense lawyers in the country, and this led to the formation of the Barone Defense Firm in 2003, which is now headquartered in Birmingham, Michigan. The Barone Defense Firm maintains offices in Grand Rapids as well.

After a national search in 2006, Patrick was offered the opportunity to become the new author of *Defending Drinking Drivers*, which was first published in 1986 and authored by one of the titans of DUI defense, John Tarantino. This two-volume textbook remains widely considered a seminal work on the subject. In 2007 Patrick took over as the executive editor of the *DWI Journal - Law and Science*, and in 2008 he was offered a position as an adjunct professor at the

Western University Cooley Law School where he teaches a course entitled "Drunk Driving Law & Practice." He has also authored chapters in *Defending DUI Vehicular Homicide Cases,* 2012/2014 eds., and a chapter in *Witness Preparation and Examination for DUI Proceedings,* 2015 ed.: *Leading Lawyers on Understanding the Role of Witnesses in DUI Cases* (Inside the Minds) *(Aspatore Books)*. In 2017 Patrick authored two more books, one entitled *Michigan Gun Law* and the book you are now holding, *The Entrepreneur's Guide to the Michigan Medical Marijuana Laws*.

In 2010 Patrick accepted a position as a legal skills instructor for the CDAM/Cooley Trial Practice College, and in 2012 he graduated from the Gerry Spence Trial Lawyer's College. In 2018 Patrick will became a Board-Certified Practitioner of Psychodrama; an action method used by many of the nation's top trial lawyers for trial preparation and presentation. No other Michigan lawyer has this distinction.

Patrick has applied his psychodrama training in his law and trial practice, in his teaching of law and trial skills, sociodrama in the business environment and Bibliodrama and psychodrama in the church setting. In his capacity as a business consultant, Patrick has worked with business owners and executives in businesses of all sizes throughout Michigan, including by way of example, TGI Direct, Movimento, AcuMax, A2 Energy Systems LLC, Spry Publishing, Compliance Training Partners/Drakeshire Dental, Booms Stone Co., The Hunter Group, LLC., Vistage Michigan, and dozens of other businesses and executives.

Patrick has an "AV" (highest) rating from Martindale-Hubbell, and since 2009 has been included in the highly selective *US News & World Report's America's Best Lawyers,* while The Barone Defense Firm appears in their companion *America's Best Law Firms*. He has been rated "Seriously Outstanding" by SuperLawyers, rated "Outstanding/10.0" by AVVO, and was appointed to the advisory board for the Michigan edition of *Leading Lawyers Magazine*.

The youngest of 6 children, Patrick grew up in Oakland County. He has been happily married for over 20 years and is the father of two girls.

Patrick can be reached on the web at: **baronedefensefirm.com**.

Contributing Author: Keith Corbett

Keith Corbett is the son of a New York Police Officer, who has been described by one of the many newspapers that featured him as, "a cocky, street-smart Irish kid from Brooklyn." After graduating in 1967 from a seminary with plans to become a priest, Keith enrolled at Canisius College in Buffalo, where he obtained a political science degree in 1971. Then, in 1974, he graduated from the Notre Dame Law School and was soon admitted to the Michigan Bar. His first government position was with the Oakland County Michigan Prosecuting Attorney's Office. Shortly after he left this position to take on a federal position, eventually becoming the Chief of the Organized Crime and Racketeering Division for the US Federal Attorney's office.

Keith was honored by receiving the Executive Director's award for "Outstanding Trial Practice" from the Executive Office of the US Attorney. Keith has tried thousands of criminal cases at both the state and federal levels. Many of these cases were extraordinarily complicated, and had dozens of boxes of evidence. Keith is also largely credited as having, in the 1990s, taken down the Detroit Mafia after he helped convict the top leaders of racketeering and other charges spanning three decades. It has been said of Keith that, "he can try cases with little preparation, yet recall key evidence with lethal precision."

Because of his superior trial strategy and record of courtroom success, Keith has been asked to teach trial tactics to attorneys at the University of Michigan School of Law and at The Department of Justice in South Carolina, Brazil, Uzbekistan, and Germany.

In His Own Words

I have been practicing law for more than 40 years now and for 35 of those years, I was a prosecutor—mostly in the federal system—for about 31 years. When I retired from government service, my area of expertise was criminal law but I didn't really feel comfortable representing drug dealers, organized crime figures, and significant criminals. So, I was looking around for something where I could use the skills I had developed as a prosecutor and trial attorney in a context that would make me feel personally comfortable. And when the opportunity to work at the Barone Defense Firm came, knowing that they specialize in DUI and OWI cases, I felt that this was an area where I can do some good.

Now with the expansion of the firm into other areas of criminal law, including health care and prescription fraud, public corruption, gun law and medical marijuana, the people we represent are solid citizens who may be falsely accused, or who may have made a poor decision one day and we do not want to see their lives ruined because of that. I believe that people shouldn't lose their entire lives for one mistake. So, I enjoy the opportunity to help people overcome a poor decision, and move on, and put themselves in a position where they can go forward with their lives. Plus, I have the luxury of being able to decide what cases to accept and which to pass on.

Mr. Corbett can be reached on the web at: **baronedefensefirm.com**.

Contributing Author: Jeff Ellis, CPA

Jeffrey Ellis is a senior tax partner in the firm of Edwards, Ellis, Stanley, Armstrong, Bowren, Krizan & Company, P.C. He was licensed a certified public accountant in 1984 and obtained a Master of Science in Taxation degree from Walsh College. Mr. Ellis has been advising clients for over 35 years on personal and business financial matters including investment evaluations, estate planning, tax planning and compliance, tax controversy resolution, business management consulting, and preparing business valuations. Mr. Ellis has experience working with clients in applying the provisions of Internal Revenue Code Section 280E and full absorption accounting for inventory. Mr. Ellis is the partner-in-charge of the tax department for the Troy and Ann Arbor offices Edwards, Ellis, Stanley, Armstrong, Bowren, Krizan & Company, P.C.

Jeff can be reached on the web at: **cpasandadvisors.com**

Contributing Author: Mark Fisher, J.D.

Contributing Author: William Honaker, J.D.

With over 25 years of experience, Bill has extensive knowledge and expertise in all aspects of patent, trademark, trade secret and copyright matters including litigation in a broad range of technologies/industries. For his clients, he evaluates patents, trademarks, and copyrights along with advising clients on the protection of inventions, trademarks, and copyrightable subject matter. Bill is a highly sought-after IP attorney in part due to his proprietary client communication and project management system, The Harmony System™.

Bill's representation includes Fortune 500 clients, small to mid-size privately held companies, and startups. He approaches each client matter from the perspective of the business—whether it is IP rights, IP infringement, or litigation. Bill listens and asks questions to fully understand the true invention and what is critical to his client's business.

Bill has the unique ability to help clients avoid unnecessary litigation. He has represented numerous clients in resolving Intellectual Property litigation in the early stages and many times before the lawsuit is even filed. Through extensive research of technologies throughout the world, he can typically find proof that the competitor's patent is not valid or substantially limited in scope. He helps clients understand the costs of litigation, both financial and personal, and the many options other than litigation that are available. In the event litigation is unavoidable, Bill utilizes a team approach putting the right person at the right cost doing the right job. With over 70 IP specialists at various rates, he can provide superior value at extremely reasonable rates.

Bill has developed the Harmony System™ to address the typical frustrations that clients have with their IP counsel. The Harmony System™ is a three-step process that covers critical ongoing information to keep clients informed and ensure there are no surprises. Bill provides regular presentations and training seminars for his clients and their employees on Intellectual Property issues of importance to their business. He also investigates his clients' businesses to better understand their business and provide relevant information to them.

Bill can be reached on the web at: **dickinson-wright.com**

Contributing Author: Danial J. McGlynn, J.D.

Daniel J. McGlynn is the Founder and Managing Partner of McGlynn Associates, PLC. Dan is a graduate of the Detroit College of Law 1992, now known as Michigan State University College of Law. He earned his B.A. from St. Louis University and graduated from the United States Marine Corps Officer Candidate School. Dan is licensed to practice law in the state of Michigan and has been admitted to practice in multiple other States of the Union, Pro Hac Vice.

Dan was elected as a member of the Governing Council of the Michigan State Bar Litigation Section in 2009, being re-elected in 2012 and continues in this capacity where he acts as Chairman of the Rules and Legislation Committee of the Council. In 2016, Dan was elected by his peers to become Secretary of the Executive Board of the Governing Council.

Dan is appointed and recognized as one of the 100 Premier Trial Attorneys in the state of Michigan for Business Law practice by The National Academy of Jurisprudence.

Dan has been a Member of the Inns of Court in Oakland County, an attorney/Judge scholarly program for the advancement of professionalism and competency in the legal profession. Additionally, he is a founder and member of the Board of Directors of the Warrior Bar Association.

Dan's over 25 years of experience in the legal field include representation in a broad space of corporate operations and activities in virtually every type of business endeavor, including industrial manufacturing, service industries, wholesale and retail and myriad other niche industries both in connection with transactional and litigation matters. He has practiced in the Michigan Court of Appeals and Supreme Court and is licensed to practice in the US Federal District Court for the Eastern District of Michigan.

Dan can be reached on the web at: **mcglynnassoc.com**

Endnotes

Index to Authorities

Chapter 1

1. Michigan Medical Marijuana Act (Section 333.26424)

    a. Protection for Medical Use of Marijuana (333.26424 section 4 (a-o)).

2. The Ogden Memo: https://www.justice.gov/opa/blog/memorandum-selected-united-state-attorneys-investigations-and-prosecutions-states

3. ACLU Complaint For Banning Marijuana: http://www.aclumich.org/sites/default/files/Lottcomplaint.pdf

4. The Cole Memo: https://www.justice.gov/iso/opa/resources/3052013829132756857467.pdf

5. *Casias v. Wal-Mart Stores, Inc.*, 764 F. Supp. 2d 914 (2011)

6. *STATE OF MICHIGAN v McQUEEN* Docket No. 143824. Argued October 11, 2012 (Calendar No. 7). Decided February 8, 2013

7. Controlled Substance Act (Title 21, Chapter 13)

8. *People v. Koon:* http://courts.mi.gov/Courts/MichiganSupremeCourt/Clerks/Recent%20Opinions/12-13-Term-Opinions/145259%20Opinion.pdf

9. *People v. Bylsma:* https://scholar.google.com/scholar_case?case=4222300144791930482&q=people+v.+bylsma&hl=en&as_sdt=400006&as_vis=1

Chapter 2

1. MCL sec. 333.26424.

2. MCL sec. 333.26428

3. *People v. Randall*, Unpublished opinion No. 318740, January 13, 2015

4. MCL sec. 333.26423(k)

5. MCL sec. 333.27501(1)(a)

6. *People v. Bylsma*, 493 Mich. 17 (2012)

7. MCL sec. 333.26423(g).

8. *People v. Ventura*, 316 Mich. App. 671 (2016)

9. MCL sec. 333.26424(l)

10. Caregiver Change Form (MMP 3502A) http://www.michigan.gov/documents/lara/LARA_BHCS_MMMP_CareGiver_Change_Form_0115_478319_7.pdf

11. Patient Change Form (MMP 3502A) http://www.michigan.gov/documents/lara/LARA_BHCS_MMMP_Patient_Change_Form_0115_478317_7.pdf

12. MMMP Minor Application Packet (MMP 3500-1 A) http://www.michigan.gov/documents/lara/lara_BHCS_MMMP_MINOR_Application_Packet_0115_478522_7.pdf

13. MMMP Application Packet (MMP 3501 A) http://www.michigan.gov/documents/lara/lara_BHCS_MMMP_Application_Packet_0115_478291_7.pdf

14. Release for Disclosure of Information Form (MMP 3000) http://www.michigan.gov/documents/lara/lara_MMP_Release_of_Information_5-13_423664_7.pdf

15. Controlled Substance Act (Title 21, Chapter 13)
16. *People v. Green*, 829 N.W. 2d 921, 299 Mich. App. 313 (2013)
17. M Crim JI 4.3
18. Id.
19. MI Crim JI 4.3 Circumstantial Evidence

Chapter 3

1. *McCoullock v. Maryland*, 17 US (4 Wheat) 316, 316 4 L. Ed 579 (1819)
2. *Pennsylvania v. Nebraska*, 350 US 497, 76 S. Ct 477, 100 L. Ed 640 (1956)
3. *Heath v. Alabama,* 472 US 82, 88, 106 S. Ct 433, 88 L. Ed 2d 387 (1985)

Chapter 4

1. 333.26421, et. seq
2. MCL 333.26423(f)
3. MCL 333.26424b
4. MCL 333.27102
5. MCL 333.26423(n)
6. 333.26423(j)
7. MCL sec. 333.26424b
8. MCL sec. 333.26424
9. MCL § 257.625, et. seq.
10. M Crim JI 15.3
11. *County of Winnebago v. Ford*, 363 Wis.2d 657 (2015)

12. *State v. Graske*, Nos.2009AP1933–CR, 2009AP1934, unpublished slip op. (WI App Mar. 24, 2010).

13. See *State v. Secrist*, 224 Wis.2d 201, 212, 589 N.W.2d 387 (1999) at 210–11 (quoting *State v. Judge*, 645 A.2d 1224, 1228 (1994)).

Chapter 5

1. Medical Marijuana Facilities Licensing Act 281 of 2016 sec. 333.27101
2. MCL sec. 333.27401
3. MCL sec. 333.27402
4. MCL sec. 333.27301-sec. 333.27305
5. MCL sec. 333.27501-27505
6. MCL sec. 333.27203
7. MCL sec. 333.27302
8. MCL sec. 333.27801
9. MCL sec. 333.27208
10. MCL sec. 333.27207
11. MCL sec. 333.27201

Chapter 6

1. MCL secs. 333.26421 - 333.26430
2. MCL secs. 333.27101 - 333.27801
3. MCL secs. 333.27901 - 333.27904
4. MCL sec. 333.27501 Grower license
5. MCL sec. 333.27502 Processor license
6. MCL sec. 333.27504 Provisioning center license

7. MCL sec. 333.27505 Safety compliance facility license
8. MCL sec. 333.27503 Secure transporter license
9. MCL secs. 333.26421 - 333.26430
10. MCL 333.27302
11. MCL sec. 333.27302(d)
12. MCL sec. 333.27601
13. MCL 333.27201

Chapter 7

1. MCL secs. 333.27101 - 333.27801
2. Id.
3. MCL sec. 333.27102(o)
4. MCL sec. 333.27402(1).
5. MCL 333.26424 and MCL sec. 333.27102(z).
6. MCL sec. 333.27409
7. Id.

Chapter 8

1. http://www.marketwired.com/press -release/michigan-awards-appriss-health-contract-fornew-prescription-monitoring-solution-2184625.htm, last checked 6.23.17
2. Section 4 of the Michigan Medical Marijuana Act, 2008 IL 1, MCL 333.26424
3. MCL sec. 333.27903(2)(d)
4. MCL sec. 333.27903(2)(c)
5. MCL sec. 333.27903(4)
6. MCL sec. Section 333.27904

Chapter 9

1. MCL sec. 333.27501(5)
2. MCL sec. 333.27502(3)
3. MCL sec. 333.27504(3)
4. MCL sec. 333.27505(3)
5. History: Const. 1963, Art. I, § 6, Eff. Jan. 1, 1964.
   Former constitution: See Const. 1908, Art. II, § 5.
6. *People v. Powell*, 303 Mich. App. 271, 842 N.W.2d 538 (2013).
7. MCL sec. 780.972
8. MCL sec. 780.951
9. 21 U.S.C. 802
10. 18 U.S.C sec. 922(g)(3)
11. See question 11e of ATF form 4473
12. , 350 Or. 299 (2011), which was an En Banc decision of the Oregon Supreme Court.
13. MCL secs. 28.421 et. seq., and MCL sec. 28.425b
14. MCL sec. 600.2950 or MCL 600.2950a.
15. MCL sec. 750.224f
16. MCL sec. 257.627a
17. MCL sec. 257.625 and sec. 257.625(9)(b)
18. MCL 257.625m, and sec. 257.625m(4).
19. MCL 324.80176
20. MCL § 28.425k(2)
21. MCL § 28.425k(8)(c)

APPENDIX A

MICHIGAN MEDICAL MARIHUANA ACT

Initiated Law 1 of 2008

AN INITIATION of Legislation to allow under state law the medical use of marihuana; to provide protections for the medical use of marihuana; to provide for a system of registry identification cards for qualifying patients and primary caregivers; to impose a fee for registry application and renewal; to make an appropriation; to provide for the promulgation of rules; to provide for the administration of this act; to provide for enforcement of this act; to provide for affirmative defenses; and to provide for penalties for violations of this act.

MICHIGAN MEDICAL MARIHUANA ACT (EXCERPT)
Initiated Law 1 of 2008

MCL § 333.26421 Short title.

Sec. 1. This act shall be known and may be cited as the Michigan Medical Marihuana Act.

MCL § 333.26422 Findings, declaration.

Sec. 2. The people of the State of Michigan find and declare that:

(a) Modern medical research, including as found by the National Academy of Sciences' Institute of Medicine in a March 1999 report, has discovered beneficial uses for marihuana in treating or alleviating the pain, nausea, and other symptoms associated with a variety of debilitating medical conditions.

(b) Data from the Federal Bureau of Investigation Uniform Crime Reports and the Compendium of Federal Justice Statistics show that approximately 99 out of every 100 marihuana arrests in the United States are made under state law, rather than under federal law. Consequently, changing state law will have the practical effect of protecting from arrest the vast majority of seriously ill people who have a medical need to use marihuana.

(c) Although federal law currently prohibits any use of marihuana except under very limited circumstances, states are not required to enforce federal law or prosecute people for engaging in activities prohibited by federal law. The laws of Alaska, California, Colorado, Hawaii, Maine, Montana, Nevada, New Mexico, Oregon, Vermont, Rhode Island, and Washington do not penalize the medical use and cultivation of marihuana. Michigan joins in this effort for the health and welfare of its citizens.

MCL § 333.26423 Definitions.

As used in this act:

(a) "Bona fide physician-patient relationship" means a treatment or counseling relationship between a physician and patient in which all of the following are present:

(1) The physician has reviewed the patient's relevant medical records and completed a full assessment of the patient's medical history and current medical condition, including a relevant, in-person, medical evaluation of the patient.

(2) The physician has created and maintained records of the patient's condition in accord with medically accepted standards.

(3) The physician has a reasonable expectation that he or she will provide follow-up care to the patient to monitor the efficacy of the use of medical marihuana as a treatment of the patient's debilitating medical condition.

(4) If the patient has given permission, the physician has notified the patient's primary care physician of the patient's debilitating medical condition and certification for the medical use of marihuana to treat that condition.

(b) "Debilitating medical condition" means 1 or more of the following:

(1) Cancer, glaucoma, positive status for human immunodeficiency virus, acquired immune deficiency syndrome, hepatitis C, amyotrophic lateral sclerosis, Crohn's disease, agitation of Alzheimer's disease, nail patella, or the treatment of these conditions.

(2) A chronic or debilitating disease or medical condition or its treatment that produces 1 or more of the following: cachexia

or wasting syndrome; severe and chronic pain; severe nausea; seizures, including but not limited to those characteristic of epilepsy; or severe and persistent muscle spasms, including but not limited to those characteristic of multiple sclerosis.

(3) Any other medical condition or its treatment approved by the department, as provided for in section 6(k).

(c) "Department" means the department of licensing and regulatory affairs.

(d) "Enclosed, locked facility" means a closet, room, or other comparable, stationary, and fully enclosed area equipped with secured locks or other functioning security devices that permit access only by a registered primary caregiver or registered qualifying patient. Marihuana plants grown outdoors are considered to be in an enclosed, locked facility if they are not visible to the unaided eye from an adjacent property when viewed by an individual at ground level or from a permanent structure and are grown within a stationary structure that is enclosed on all sides, except for the base, by chain-link fencing, wooden slats, or a similar material that prevents access by the general public and that is anchored, attached, or affixed to the ground; located on land that is owned, leased, or rented by either the registered qualifying patient or a person designated through the departmental registration process as the primary caregiver for the registered qualifying patient or patients for whom the marihuana plants are grown; and equipped with functioning locks or other security devices that restrict access to only the registered qualifying patient or the registered primary caregiver who owns, leases, or rents the property on which the structure is located. Enclosed, locked facility includes a motor vehicle if both of the following conditions are met:

(1) The vehicle is being used temporarily to transport living marihuana plants from 1 location to another with the intent to permanently retain those plants at the second location.

(2) An individual is not inside the vehicle unless he or she is either the registered qualifying patient to whom the living marihuana plants belong or the individual designated through the departmental registration process as the primary caregiver for the registered qualifying patient.

(e) "Marihuana" means that term as defined in section 7106 of the public health code, 1978 PA 368, MCL 333.7106.

(f) "Marihuana-infused product" means a topical formulation, tincture, beverage, edible substance, or similar product containing any usable marihuana that is intended for human consumption in a manner other than smoke inhalation. Marihuana-infused product shall not be considered a food for purposes of the food law, 2000 PA 92, MCL 289.1101 to 289.8111.

(g) "Marihuana plant" means any plant of the species Cannabis sativa L.

(h) "Medical use of marihuana" means the acquisition, possession, cultivation, manufacture, extraction, use, internal possession, delivery, transfer, or transportation of marihuana, marihuana-infused products, or paraphernalia relating to the administration of marihuana to treat or alleviate a registered qualifying patient's debilitating medical condition or symptoms associated with the debilitating medical condition.

(i) "Physician" means an individual licensed as a physician under part 170 of the public health code, 1978 PA 368, MCL 333.17001 to 333.17084, or an osteopathic physician under part 175 of the public health code, 1978 PA 368, MCL 333.17501 to 333.17556.

(j) "Plant" means any living organism that produces its own food through photosynthesis and has observable root formation or is in growth material.

(k) "Primary caregiver" or "caregiver" means a person who is at least 21 years old and who has agreed to assist with a patient's medical use of marihuana and who has not been convicted of any felony within the past 10 years and has never been convicted of a felony involving illegal drugs or a felony that is an assaultive crime as defined in section 9a of chapter X of the code of criminal procedure, 1927 PA 175, MCL 770.9a.

(l) "Qualifying patient" or "patient" means a person who has been diagnosed by a physician as having a debilitating medical condition.

(m) "Registry identification card" means a document issued by the department that identifies a person as a registered qualifying patient or registered primary caregiver.

(n) "Usable marihuana" means the dried leaves, flowers, plant resin, or extract of the marihuana plant, but does not include the seeds, stalks, and roots of the plant.

(o) "Usable marihuana equivalent" means the amount of usable marihuana in a marihuana-infused product that is calculated as provided in section 4(c).

(p) "Visiting qualifying patient" means a patient who is not a resident of this state or who has been a resident of this state for less than 30 days.

(q) "Written certification" means a document signed by a physician, stating all of the following:

(1) The patient's debilitating medical condition.

(2) The physician has completed a full assessment of the patient's medical history and current medical condition, including a relevant, in-person, medical evaluation.

(3) In the physician's professional opinion, the patient is likely to receive therapeutic or palliative benefit from the medical use of marihuana to treat or alleviate the patient's debilitating medical condition or symptoms associated with the debilitating medical condition.

MCL § 333.26424 Qualifying patient or primary caregiver; arrest, prosecution, or penalty prohibited; conditions; privilege from arrests; presumption; compensation; physician subject to arrest, prosecution, or penalty prohibited; marihuana paraphernalia; person in presence or vicinity of medical use of marihuana; registry identification card issued outside of department; sale of marihuana as felony; penalty; marihuana-infused product.

(a) A qualifying patient who has been issued and possesses a registry identification card is not subject to arrest, prosecution, or penalty in any manner, or denied any right or privilege, including, but not limited to, civil penalty or disciplinary action by a business or occupational or professional licensing board or bureau, for the medical use of marihuana in accordance with this act, provided that the qualifying patient possesses an amount of marihuana that does not exceed a combined total of 2.5 ounces of usable marihuana and usable marihuana equivalents, and, if the qualifying patient has not specified that a primary caregiver will be allowed under state law to cultivate marihuana for the qualifying patient, 12 marihuana plants kept in an enclosed, locked facility. Any incidental amount of seeds, stalks, and unusable roots shall also be allowed under state law and shall not be included in this amount. The privilege from arrest under this subsection applies only if the qualifying patient presents both his or her registry identification card and a valid driver license or government-issued identification card that bears a photographic image of the qualifying patient.

(b) A primary caregiver who has been issued and possesses a registry identification card is not subject to arrest, prosecution, or penalty in any manner, or denied any right or privilege, including but not limited to civil penalty or disciplinary action by a business or occupational or professional licensing board or bureau, for assisting a qualifying patient to whom he or she is connected through the department's registration process with the medical use of marihuana in accordance with this act. The privilege from arrest under this subsection applies only if the primary caregiver presents both his or her registry identification card and a valid driver license or government-issued identification card that bears a photographic image of the primary caregiver. This subsection applies only if the primary caregiver possesses marihuana in forms and amounts that do not exceed any of the following:

(1) For each qualifying patient to whom he or she is connected through the department's registration process, a combined total of 2.5 ounces of usable marihuana and usable marihuana equivalents.

(2) For each registered qualifying patient who has specified that the primary caregiver will be allowed under state law to cultivate marihuana for the qualifying patient, 12 marihuana plants kept in an enclosed, locked facility.

(3) Any incidental amount of seeds, stalks, and unusable roots.

(c) For purposes of determining usable marihuana equivalency, the following shall be considered equivalent to 1 ounce of usable marihuana:

(1) 16 ounces of marihuana-infused product if in a solid form.

(2) 7 grams of marihuana-infused product if in a gaseous form.

(3) 36 fluid ounces of marihuana-infused product if in a liquid form.

(d) A person shall not be denied custody or visitation of a minor for acting in accordance with this act, unless the person's behavior is such that it creates an unreasonable danger to the minor that can be clearly articulated and substantiated.

(e) There is a presumption that a qualifying patient or primary caregiver is engaged in the medical use of marihuana in accordance with this act if the qualifying patient or primary caregiver complies with both of the following:

(1) Is in possession of a registry identification card.

(2) Is in possession of an amount of marihuana that does not exceed the amount allowed under this act. The presumption may be rebutted by evidence that conduct related to marihuana was not for the purpose of alleviating the qualifying patient's debilitating medical condition or symptoms associated with the debilitating medical condition, in accordance with this act.

(f) A registered primary caregiver may receive compensation for costs associated with assisting a registered qualifying patient in the medical use of marihuana. Any such compensation does not constitute the sale of controlled substances.

(g) A physician shall not be subject to arrest, prosecution, or penalty in any manner, or denied any right or privilege, including but not limited to civil penalty or disciplinary action by the Michigan board of medicine, the Michigan board of osteopathic medicine and surgery, or any other business or occupational or professional licensing board or bureau, solely for providing written certifications, in the course of a bona fide physician-patient relationship and after the physician has completed a full assessment of the qualifying patient's medical history, or for otherwise stating that, in the physician's professional opinion, a patient is likely to receive therapeutic or palliative benefit from the medical use of marihuana to treat or alleviate the patient's serious or debilitating medical condition or symptoms associated with the serious or debilitating medical condition, provided that nothing shall prevent a professional licensing board from sanctioning a physician for failing to properly evaluate a patient's medical condition or otherwise violating the standard of care for evaluating medical conditions.

(h) A person shall not be subject to arrest, prosecution, or penalty in any manner, or denied any right or privilege, including but not limited to civil penalty or disciplinary action by a business or occupational or professional licensing board or bureau, for providing a registered qualifying patient or a registered primary caregiver with marihuana paraphernalia for purposes of a qualifying patient's medical use of marihuana.

(i) Any marihuana, marihuana paraphernalia, or licit property that is possessed, owned, or used in connection with the medical use of marihuana, as allowed under this act, or acts incidental to such use, shall not be seized or forfeited.

(j) A person shall not be subject to arrest, prosecution, or penalty in any manner, or denied any right or privilege, including but not limited to civil penalty or disciplinary action by a business or occupational or professional licensing board or bureau, solely for being in the presence or vicinity of the medical use of marihuana in accordance with this act, or for assisting a registered qualifying patient with using or administering marihuana.

(k) A registry identification card, or its equivalent, that is issued under the laws of another state, district, territory, commonwealth, or insular possession of the United States that allows the medical use of marihuana by a visiting qualifying patient, or to allow a person to assist with a visiting qualifying patient's medical use of marihuana, shall have the same force and effect as a registry identification card issued by the department.

(l) Any registered qualifying patient or registered primary caregiver who sells marihuana to someone who is not allowed the medical use of marihuana under this act shall have his or her registry identification card revoked and is guilty of a felony punishable by imprisonment for not more than 2 years or a fine of not more than $2,000.00, or both, in addition to any other penalties for the distribution of marihuana.

(m) A person shall not be subject to arrest, prosecution, or penalty in any manner or denied any right or privilege, including, but not limited to, civil penalty or disciplinary action by a business or occupational or professional licensing board or bureau, for manufacturing a marihuana-infused product if the person is any of the following:

(1) A registered qualifying patient, manufacturing for his or her own personal use.

(2) A registered primary caregiver, manufacturing for the use of a patient to whom he or she is connected through the department's registration process.

(n) A qualifying patient shall not transfer a marihuana-infused product or marihuana to any individual.

(o) A primary caregiver shall not transfer a marihuana-infused product to any individual who is not a qualifying patient to whom he or she is connected through the department's registration process.

MCL § 333.26424a Registered qualifying patient or registered primary caregiver; arrest, prosecution, or penalty, or denial of right or privilege prohibited; conditions.

(1) This section does not apply unless the medical marihuana facilities licensing act is enacted.

(2) A registered qualifying patient or registered primary caregiver shall not be subject to arrest, prosecution, or penalty in any manner, or denied any right or privilege, including, but not limited to, civil penalty or disciplinary action by a business or occupational or professional licensing board or bureau, for any of the following:

(a) Transferring or purchasing marihuana in an amount authorized by this act from a provisioning center licensed under the medical marihuana facilities licensing act.

(b) Transferring or selling marihuana seeds or seedlings to a grower licensed under the medical marihuana facilities licensing act.

(c) Transferring marihuana for testing to and from a safety compliance facility licensed under the medical marihuana facilities licensing act.

MCL § 333.26424b Transporting or possessing marihuana-infused product; violation; fine.

(1) Except as provided in subsections (2) to (4), a qualifying patient or primary caregiver shall not transport or possess a marihuana-infused product in or upon a motor vehicle.

(2) This section does not prohibit a qualifying patient from transporting or possessing a marihuana-infused product in or upon a motor vehicle if the marihuana-infused product is in a sealed and labeled package that is carried in the trunk of the vehicle or, if the vehicle does not have a trunk, is carried so as not to be readily accessible from the interior of the vehicle. The label must state the weight of the marihuana-infused product in ounces, name of the manufacturer, date of manufacture, name of the person from whom the marihuana-infused product was received, and date of receipt.

(3) This section does not prohibit a primary caregiver from transporting or possessing a marihuana-infused product in or upon a motor vehicle if the marihuana-infused product is accompanied by an accurate marihuana transportation manifest and enclosed in a case carried in the trunk of the vehicle or, if the vehicle does not have a trunk, is enclosed in a case and carried so as not to be readily accessible from the interior of the vehicle. The manifest form must state the weight of each marihuana-infused product in ounces, name and address of the manufacturer, date of manufacture, destination name and address, date and time of departure, estimated date and time of arrival, and, if applicable, name and address of the person from whom the product was received and date of receipt.

(4) This section does not prohibit a primary caregiver from transporting or possessing a marihuana-infused product in or upon a motor vehicle for the use of his or her child, spouse, or parent who is a qualifying patient if the marihuana-infused product is in a sealed and labeled package that is carried in the trunk of the vehicle or, if the vehicle does not have a trunk, is carried so as not to be readily accessible from the interior of the vehicle. The label must state the weight of the marihuana-infused product in ounces, name of the manufacturer, date of manufacture, name of the qualifying patient, and, if applicable, name of the person from whom the marihuana-infused product was received and date of receipt.

(5) For purposes of determining compliance with quantity limitations under section 4, there is a rebuttable presumption that the weight of a marihuana-infused product listed on its package label or on a marihuana transportation manifest is accurate.

(6) A qualifying patient or primary caregiver who violates this section is responsible for a civil fine of not more than $250.00.

MCL § 333.26425 Rules.

(a) Not later than 120 days after the effective date of this act, the department shall promulgate rules pursuant to the administrative procedures act of 1969, 1969 PA 306, MCL 24.201 to 24.328, that govern the manner in which the department shall consider the addition of medical conditions or treatments to the list of debilitating medical conditions set forth in section 3(a) of this act. In promulgating rules, the department shall allow for petition by the public to include additional medical conditions and treatments. In considering such petitions, the department shall include public notice of, and an opportunity to comment in a public hearing upon, such petitions. The department shall, after hearing, approve or deny such petitions within 180 days of the submission of the petition. The approval or denial of such a petition shall be considered a final department action, subject to judicial review pursuant to the administrative procedures act of 1969, 1969 PA 306, MCL 24.201 to 24.328. Jurisdiction and venue for judicial review are vested in the circuit court for the county of Ingham.

(b) Not later than 120 days after the effective date of this act, the department shall promulgate rules pursuant to the administrative procedures act of 1969, 1969 PA 306, MCL 24.201 to 24.328, that govern the manner in which it shall consider applications for and renewals of registry identification cards for qualifying patients and primary caregivers. The department's rules shall establish application and renewal fees that generate revenues sufficient to offset all expenses of implementing and administering this act. The department may establish a sliding scale of application and renewal fees based upon a qualifying patient's family income. The department may accept gifts, grants, and other donations from private sources in order to reduce the application and renewal fees.

MCL § 333.26426 Administration and enforcement of rules by department.

(a) The department shall issue registry identification cards to qualifying patients who submit the following, in accordance with the department's rules:

(1) A written certification;

(2) Application or renewal fee;

(3) Name, address, and date of birth of the qualifying patient, except that if the applicant is homeless, no address is required;

(4) Name, address, and telephone number of the qualifying patient's physician;

(5) Name, address, and date of birth of the qualifying patient's primary caregiver, if any;

(6) Proof of Michigan residency. For the purposes of this subdivision, a person shall be considered to have proved legal residency in this state if any of the following apply:

(i) The person provides a copy of a valid, lawfully obtained Michigan driver license issued under the Michigan vehicle code, 1949 PA 300, MCL 257.1 to 257.923, or an official state personal identification card issued under 1972 PA 222, MCL 28.291 to 28.300.

(ii) The person provides a copy of a valid Michigan voter registration.

(7) If the qualifying patient designates a primary caregiver, a designation as to whether the qualifying patient or primary

caregiver will be allowed under state law to possess marihuana plants for the qualifying patient's medical use.

(b) The department shall not issue a registry identification card to a qualifying patient who is under the age of 18 unless:

(1) The qualifying patient's physician has explained the potential risks and benefits of the medical use of marihuana to the qualifying patient and to his or her parent or legal guardian;

(2) The qualifying patient's parent or legal guardian submits a written certification from 2 physicians; and

(3) The qualifying patient's parent or legal guardian consents in writing to:

(A) Allow the qualifying patient's medical use of marihuana;

(B) Serve as the qualifying patient's primary caregiver; and

(C) Control the acquisition of the marihuana, the dosage, and the frequency of the medical use of marihuana by the qualifying patient.

(c) The department shall verify the information contained in an application or renewal submitted pursuant to this section, and shall approve or deny an application or renewal within 15 business days of receiving it. The department may deny an application or renewal only if the applicant did not provide the information required pursuant to this section, or if the department determines that the information provided was falsified. Rejection of an application or renewal is considered a final department action, subject to judicial review. Jurisdiction and venue for judicial review are vested in the circuit court for the county of Ingham.

(d) The department shall issue a registry identification card to the primary caregiver, if any, who is named in a qualifying patient's approved application; provided that each qualifying patient can have no more than 1 primary caregiver, and a primary caregiver may assist no more than 5 qualifying patients with their medical use of marihuana.

(e) The department shall issue registry identification cards within 5 business days of approving an application or renewal, which shall expire 2 years after the date of issuance. Registry identification cards shall contain all of the following:

(1) Name, address, and date of birth of the qualifying patient.

(2) Name, address, and date of birth of the primary caregiver, if any, of the qualifying patient.

(3) The date of issuance and expiration date of the registry identification card.

(4) A random identification number.

(5) A photograph, if the department requires one by rule.

(6) A clear designation showing whether the primary caregiver or the qualifying patient will be allowed under state law to possess the marihuana plants for the qualifying patient's medical use, which shall be determined based solely on the qualifying patient's preference.

(f) If a registered qualifying patient's certifying physician notifies the department in writing that the patient has ceased to suffer from a debilitating medical condition, the card shall become null and void upon notification by the department to the patient.

(g) Possession of, or application for, a registry identification card shall not constitute probable cause or reasonable suspicion, nor shall it be used to support the search of the person or property of the person possessing or applying for the registry identification card, or otherwise subject the person or property of the person to inspection by any local, county or state governmental agency.

(h) The following confidentiality rules shall apply:

(1) Subject to subdivisions (3) and (4), applications and supporting information submitted by qualifying patients, including information regarding their primary caregivers and physicians, are confidential.

(2) The department shall maintain a confidential list of the persons to whom the department has issued registry identification cards. Except as provided in subdivisions (3) and (4), individual names and other identifying information on the list are confidential and are exempt from disclosure under the freedom of information act, 1976 PA 442, MCL 15.231 to 15.246.

(3) The department shall verify to law enforcement personnel and to the necessary database created in the marihuana tracking act as established by the medical marihuana facilities licensing act whether a registry identification card is valid, without disclosing more information than is reasonably necessary to verify the authenticity of the registry identification card.

(4) A person, including an employee, contractor, or official of the department or another state agency or local unit of government, who discloses confidential information in violation of this act is guilty of a misdemeanor, punishable by imprisonment for not more than 6 months, or a fine of not more than $1,000.00, or both. Notwithstanding this provision, department employees may notify law enforcement about falsified or fraudulent information submitted to the department.

(i) The department shall submit to the legislature an annual report that does not disclose any identifying information about qualifying patients, primary caregivers, or physicians, but does contain, at a minimum, all of the following information:

(1) The number of applications filed for registry identification cards.

(2) The number of qualifying patients and primary caregivers approved in each county.

(3) The nature of the debilitating medical conditions of the qualifying patients.

(4) The number of registry identification cards revoked.

(5) The number of physicians providing written certifications for qualifying patients.

(j) The department may enter into a contract with a private contractor to assist the department in performing its duties under this section. The contract may provide for assistance in processing and issuing registry identification cards, but the department shall retain the authority to make the final determination as to issuing the registry identification card. Any contract shall include a provision requiring the contractor to preserve the confidentiality of information in conformity with subsection (h).

(k) Not later than 6 months after the effective date of the amendatory act that added this subsection, the department shall appoint a panel to review petitions to approve medical conditions or treatments for addition to the list of debilitating medical conditions under the administrative rules. The panel shall meet at least twice each year and shall review and make a recommendation to the department concerning any petitions that have been submitted that are completed and include any documentation required by administrative rule.

(1) A majority of the panel members shall be licensed physicians, and the panel shall provide recommendations to the department regarding whether the petitions should be approved or denied.

(2) All meetings of the panel are subject to the open meetings act, 1976 PA 267, MCL 15.261 to 15.275.

(l) The marihuana registry fund is created within the state treasury. All fees collected under this act shall be deposited into the fund. The state treasurer may receive money or other assets from any source for deposit into the fund. The state treasurer shall direct the investment of the fund. The state treasurer shall credit to the fund interest and earnings from fund investments. Money in the fund at the close of the fiscal year shall remain in the fund and shall not lapse to the general fund. The department of licensing and regulatory affairs shall be the administrator of the fund for auditing purposes. The department shall expend money from the fund, upon appropriation, for the operation and oversight of the Michigan medical marihuana program. For the fiscal year ending September 30, 2016, $8,500,000.00 is appropriated from the marihuana registry fund to the department for its initial costs of implementing the medical marihuana facilities licensing act and the marihuana tracking act.

MCL § 333.26427 Scope of act; limitations.

(a) The medical use of marihuana is allowed under state law to the extent that it is carried out in accordance with the provisions of this act.

(b) This act does not permit any person to do any of the following:

(1) Undertake any task under the influence of marihuana, when doing so would constitute negligence or professional malpractice.

(2) Possess marihuana, or otherwise engage in the medical use of marihuana at any of the following locations:

(A) In a school bus.

(B) On the grounds of any preschool or primary or secondary school.

(C) In any correctional facility.

(3) Smoke marihuana at any of the following locations:

(A) On any form of public transportation.

(B) In any public place.

(4) Operate, navigate, or be in actual physical control of any motor vehicle, aircraft, snowmobile, off-road recreational vehicle, or motorboat while under the influence of marihuana.

(5) Use marihuana if that person does not have a serious or debilitating medical condition.

(6) Separate plant resin from a marihuana plant by butane extraction in any public place or motor vehicle, or inside or within the curtilage of any residential structure.

(7) Separate plant resin from a marihuana plant by butane extraction in a manner that demonstrates a failure to exercise reasonable care or reckless disregard for the safety of others.

(c) Nothing in this act shall be construed to require any of the following:

(1) A government medical assistance program or commercial or non-profit health insurer to reimburse a person for costs associated with the medical use of marihuana.

(2) An employer to accommodate the ingestion of marihuana in any workplace or any employee working while under the influence of marihuana.

(3) A private property owner to lease residential property to any person who smokes or cultivates marihuana on the premises, if the prohibition against smoking or cultivating marihuana is in the written lease.

(d) Fraudulent representation to a law enforcement official of any fact or circumstance relating to the medical use of marihuana to avoid arrest or prosecution is punishable by a fine of $500.00, which is in addition to any other penalties that may apply for making a false statement or for the use of marihuana other than use undertaken pursuant to this act.

(e) All other acts and parts of acts inconsistent with this act do not apply to the medical use of marihuana as provided for by this act.

MCL § 333.26428 Defenses.

(a) Except as provided in section 7(b), a patient and a patient's primary caregiver, if any, may assert the medical purpose for using marihuana as a defense to any prosecution involving marihuana, and this defense shall be presumed valid where the evidence shows that:

(1) A physician has stated that, in the physician's professional opinion, after having completed a full assessment of the patient's

medical history and current medical condition made in the course of a bona fide physician-patient relationship, the patient is likely to receive therapeutic or palliative benefit from the medical use of marihuana to treat or alleviate the patient's serious or debilitating medical condition or symptoms of the patient's serious or debilitating medical condition;

(2) The patient and the patient's primary caregiver, if any, were collectively in possession of a quantity of marihuana that was not more than was reasonably necessary to ensure the uninterrupted availability of marihuana for the purpose of treating or alleviating the patient's serious or debilitating medical condition or symptoms of the patient's serious or debilitating medical condition; and

(3) The patient and the patient's primary caregiver, if any, were engaged in the acquisition, possession, cultivation, manufacture, use, delivery, transfer, or transportation of marihuana or paraphernalia relating to the use of marihuana to treat or alleviate the patient's serious or debilitating medical condition or symptoms of the patient's serious or debilitating medical condition.

(b) A person may assert the medical purpose for using marihuana in a motion to dismiss, and the charges shall be dismissed following an evidentiary hearing where the person shows the elements listed in subsection (a).

(c) If a patient or a patient's primary caregiver demonstrates the patient's medical purpose for using marihuana pursuant to this section, the patient and the patient's primary caregiver shall not be subject to the following for the patient's medical use of marihuana:

(1) disciplinary action by a business or occupational or professional licensing board or bureau; or

(2) forfeiture of any interest in or right to property.

MCL § 333.26429 Failure of department to adopt rules or issue valid registry identification card.

(a) If the department fails to adopt rules to implement this act within 120 days of the effective date of this act, a qualifying patient may commence an action in the circuit court for the county of Ingham to compel the department to perform the actions mandated pursuant to the provisions of this act.

(b) If the department fails to issue a valid registry identification card in response to a valid application or renewal submitted pursuant to this act within 20 days of its submission, the registry identification card shall be deemed granted, and a copy of the registry identification application or renewal shall be deemed a valid registry identification card.

(c) If at any time after the 140 days following the effective date of this act the department is not accepting applications, including if it has not created rules allowing qualifying patients to submit applications, a notarized statement by a qualifying patient containing the information required in an application, pursuant to section 6(a)(3)-(6) together with a written certification, shall be deemed a valid registry identification card.

MCL § 333.26430 Severabilty.

Any section of this act being held invalid as to any person or circumstances shall not affect the application of any other section of this act that can be given full effect without the invalid section or application.

APPENDIX B

MEDICAL MARIHUANA FACILITIES LICENSING ACT

Act 281 of 2016

AN ACT to license and regulate medical marihuana growers, processors, provisioning centers, secure transporters, and safety compliance facilities; to provide for the powers and duties of certain state and local governmental officers and entities; to create a medical marihuana licensing board; to provide for interaction with the statewide monitoring system for commercial marihuana transactions; to create an advisory panel; to provide immunity from prosecution for marihuana-related offenses for persons engaging in marihuana-related activities in compliance with this act; to prescribe civil fines and sanctions and provide remedies; to provide for forfeiture of contraband; to provide for taxes, fees, and assessments; and to require the promulgation of rules.

MCL § 333.27101 Short title.

This act shall be known and may be cited as the "medical marihuana facilities licensing act".

MCL § 333.27102 Definitions.

As used in this act:

(a) "Advisory panel" or "panel" means the marihuana advisory panel created in section 801.

(b) "Affiliate" means any person that controls, is controlled by, or is under common control with; is in a partnership or joint venture relationship with; or is a co-shareholder of a corporation, a co-member of a limited liability company, or a co-partner in a limited liability partnership with a licensee or applicant.

(c) "Applicant" means a person who applies for a state operating license. With respect to disclosures in an application, or for purposes of ineligibility for a license under section 402, the term applicant includes an officer, director, and managerial employee of the applicant and a person who holds any direct or indirect ownership interest in the applicant.

(d) "Board" means the medical marihuana licensing board created in section 301.

(e) "Department" means the department of licensing and regulatory affairs.

(f) "Grower" means a licensee that is a commercial entity located in this state that cultivates, dries, trims, or cures and packages marihuana for sale to a processor or provisioning center.

(g) "Licensee" means a person holding a state operating license.

(h) "Marihuana" means that term as defined in section 7106 of the public health code, 1978 PA 368, MCL 333.7106.

(i) "Marihuana facility" means a location at which a license holder is licensed to operate under this act.

(j) "Marihuana plant" means any plant of the species Cannabis sativa L.

(k) "Marihuana-infused product" means a topical formulation, tincture, beverage, edible substance, or similar product containing any usable marihuana that is intended for human consumption in a manner other than smoke inhalation. Marihuana-infused product shall not be considered a food for purposes of the food law, 2000 PA 92, MCL 289.1101 to 289.8111.

(l) "Michigan medical marihuana act" means the Michigan medical marihuana act, 2008 IL 1, MCL 333.26421 to 333.26430.

(m) "Municipality" means a city, township, or village.

(n) "Paraphernalia" means any equipment, product, or material of any kind that is designed for or used in growing, cultivating, producing, manufacturing, compounding, converting, storing, processing, preparing, transporting, injecting, smoking, ingesting, inhaling, or otherwise introducing into the human body, marihuana.

(o) "Person" means an individual, corporation, limited liability company, partnership, limited partnership, limited liability partnership, limited liability limited partnership, trust, or other legal entity.

(p) "Plant" means any living organism that produces its own food through photosynthesis and has observable root formation or is in growth material.

(q) "Processor" means a licensee that is a commercial entity located in this state that purchases marihuana from a grower and that extracts resin from the marihuana or creates a marihuana-infused product for sale and transfer in packaged form to a provisioning center.

(r) "Provisioning center" means a licensee that is a commercial entity located in this state that purchases marihuana from a grower or processor and sells, supplies, or provides marihuana to registered qualifying patients, directly or through the patients' registered primary caregivers. Provisioning center includes any commercial property where marihuana is sold at retail to registered qualifying patients or registered primary caregivers. A noncommercial location used by a primary caregiver to assist a qualifying patient connected to the caregiver through the department's marihuana registration process in accordance with the Michigan medical marihuana act is not a provisioning center for purposes of this act.

(s) "Registered primary caregiver" means a primary caregiver who has been issued a current registry identification card under the Michigan medical marihuana act.

(t) "Registered qualifying patient" means a qualifying patient who has been issued a current registry identification card under the Michigan medical marihuana act or a visiting qualifying patient as that term is defined in section 3 of the Michigan medical marihuana act, MCL 333.26423.

(u) "Registry identification card" means that term as defined in section 3 of the Michigan medical marihuana act, MCL 333.26423.

(v) "Rules" means rules promulgated under the administrative procedures act of 1969, 1969 PA 306, MCL 24.201 to 24.328, by the department in consultation with the board to implement this act.

(w) "Safety compliance facility" means a licensee that is a commercial entity that receives marihuana from a marihuana facility or registered primary caregiver, tests it for contaminants and for tetrahydrocannabinol and other cannabinoids, returns the test results, and may return the marihuana to the marihuana facility.

(x) "Secure transporter" means a licensee that is a commercial entity located in this state that stores marihuana and transports marihuana between marihuana facilities for a fee.

(y) "State operating license" or, unless the context requires a different meaning, "license" means a license that is issued under this act that allows the licensee to operate as 1 of the following, specified in the license:

(i) A grower.

(ii) A processor.

(iii) A secure transporter.

(iv) A provisioning center.

(v) A safety compliance facility.

(z) "Statewide monitoring system" or, unless the context requires a different meaning, "system" means an internet-based, statewide database established, implemented, and maintained by the department under the marihuana tracking act, that is available to licensees, law enforcement agencies, and authorized state departments and agencies on a 24-hour basis for all of the following:

(i) Verifying registry identification cards.

(ii) Tracking marihuana transfer and transportation by licensees, including transferee, date, quantity, and price.

(iii) Verifying in commercially reasonable time that a transfer will not exceed the limit that the patient or caregiver is authorized to receive under section 4 of the Michigan medical marihuana act, MCL 333.26424.

(aa) "Usable marihuana" means the dried leaves, flowers, plant resin, or extract of the marihuana plant, but does not include the seeds, stalks, and roots of the plant.

MCL § 333.27401 Licensure; application; background investigation; consent to inspections, examinations, searches, and seizures; disclosure of confidential records; interest in other state operating license; fee; additional costs; notification to municipality.

(1) Beginning 360 days after the effective date of this act, a person may apply to the board for state operating licenses in the categories of class A, B, or C grower; processor; provisioning center; secure transporter; and safety compliance facility as provided in this act. The application shall be made under oath on a form provided by the board and shall contain information as prescribed by the board, including, but not limited to, all of the following:

(a) The name, business address, business telephone number, social security number, and, if applicable, federal tax identification number of the applicant.

(b) The identity of every person having any ownership interest in the applicant with respect to which the license is sought. If the disclosed entity is a trust, the application shall disclose the names and addresses of the beneficiaries; if a corporation, the names and addresses of all shareholders, officers, and directors; if a partnership or limited liability partnership, the names and addresses of all partners; if a limited partnership or limited liability limited partnership, the names of all partners, both general and limited; or if a limited liability company, the names and addresses of all members and managers.

(c) An identification of any business that is directly or indirectly involved in the growing, processing, testing, transporting, or sale of marihuana, including, if applicable, the state of incorporation or registration, in which an applicant or, if the applicant is an individual, the applicant's spouse, parent, or child has any equity interest. If an applicant is a corporation, partnership, or other business entity, the applicant shall identify any other corporation, partnership, or other business entity that is directly or indirectly involved in the growing, processing, testing, transporting, or sale of marihuana in which it has any equity interest, including, if applicable, the state of incorporation or registration. An applicant may comply with this subdivision by filing a copy of the applicant's registration with the Securities and Exchange Commission if the registration contains the information required by this subdivision.

(d) Whether an applicant has been indicted for, charged with, arrested for, or convicted of, pled guilty or nolo contendere to, forfeited bail concerning any criminal offense under the laws of any jurisdiction, either felony or controlled-substance-related misdemeanor, not including traffic violations, regardless of whether the offense has been reversed on appeal or otherwise, including the date, the name and location of the court, arresting agency, and prosecuting agency, the case caption, the docket number, the offense, the disposition, and the location and length of incarceration.

(e) Whether an applicant has ever applied for or has been granted any commercial license or certificate issued by a licensing authority in Michigan or any other jurisdiction that has been denied, restricted, suspended, revoked, or not renewed and a statement describing the facts and circumstances concerning the application, denial, restriction, suspension, revocation, or nonrenewal, including the licensing authority, the date each action was taken, and the reason for each action.

(f) Whether an applicant has filed, or been served with, a complaint or other notice filed with any public body, regarding the delinquency in the payment of, or a dispute over the filings concerning the payment of, any tax required under federal, state, or local law, including the amount, type of tax, taxing agency, and time periods involved.

(g) A statement listing the names and titles of all public officials or officers of any unit of government, and the spouses, parents, and children of those public officials or officers, who, directly or indirectly, own any financial interest in, have any beneficial interest in, are the creditors of or hold any debt instrument issued by, or hold or have any interest in any contractual or service relationship with an applicant. As used in this subdivision, public official or officer does not include a person who would have to be listed solely because of his or her state or federal military service.

(h) A description of the type of marihuana facility; anticipated or actual number of employees; and projected or actual gross receipts.

(i) Financial information in the manner and form prescribed by the board.

(j) A paper copy or electronic posting website reference for the ordinance or zoning restriction that the municipality adopted to authorize or restrict operation of 1 or more marihuana facilities in the municipality.

(k) A copy of the notice informing the municipality by registered mail that the applicant has applied for a license under this act. The applicant shall also certify that it has delivered the notice to the municipality or will do so by 10 days after the date the applicant submits the application for a license to the board.

(l) Any other information the department requires by rule.

(2) The board shall use information provided on the application as a basis to conduct a thorough background investigation on the applicant. A false application is cause for the board to deny a license. The board shall not consider an incomplete application but shall, within a reasonable time, return the application to the applicant with notification of the deficiency and instructions for submitting a corrected application. Information the board obtains from the background investigation is exempt from disclosure under the freedom of information act, 1976 PA 442, MCL 15.231 to 15.246.

(3) An applicant must provide written consent to the inspections, examinations, searches, and seizures provided for in section 303(1)(c)(i) to (iv) and to disclosure to the board and its agents of otherwise confidential records, including tax records held by any federal, state, or local agency, or credit bureau or financial institution, while applying for or holding a license. Information the board receives under this subsection is exempt from disclosure under the freedom of information act, 1976 PA 442, MCL 15.231 to 15.246.

(4) An applicant must certify that the applicant does not have an interest in any other state operating license that is prohibited under this act.

(5) A nonrefundable application fee must be paid at the time of filing to defray the costs associated with the background investigation conducted by the board. The department in consultation with the board shall set the amount of the application fee for each category and class of license by rule. If the costs of the investigation and processing the application exceed the application fee, the applicant shall pay the additional amount to the board. All information, records, interviews, reports, statements, memoranda, or other data supplied to or used by the board in the course of its review or investigation of an application for a license under this act shall be disclosed only in accordance with this act. The information, records, interviews, reports, statements, memoranda, or other data

are not admissible as evidence or discoverable in any action of any kind in any court or before any tribunal, board, agency, or person, except for any action considered necessary by the board.

(6) By 10 days after the date the applicant submits an application to the board, the applicant shall notify the municipality by registered mail that it has applied for a license under this act.

MCL § 333.27402 License; issuance; ineligibility; circumstances; other considerations granting license; photograph and fingerprints; fingerprint processing fee; criminal history check; requirements applicable to fingerprints; definitions; review of application; informing applicant of decision; issuance; duration; renewal; notice; expiration; consent to inspections; examinations, searches, and seizures; information required to be provided by applicant.

Sec. 402.

(1) The board shall issue a license to an applicant who submits a complete application and pays both the nonrefundable application fee required under section 401(5) and the regulatory assessment established by the board for the first year of operation, if the board determines that the applicant is qualified to receive a license under this act.

(2) An applicant is ineligible to receive a license if any of the following circumstances exist:

(a) The applicant has been convicted of or released from incarceration for a felony under the laws of this state, any other state, or the United States within the past 10 years or has been convicted of a controlled substance-related felony within the past 10 years.

(b) Within the past 5 years the applicant has been convicted of a misdemeanor involving a controlled substance, theft, dishonesty, or fraud in any state or been found responsible for violating a local ordinance in any state involving a controlled substance, dishonesty, theft, or fraud that substantially corresponds to a misdemeanor in that state.

(c) The applicant has knowingly submitted an application for a license under this act that contains false information.

(d) The applicant is a member of the board.

(e) The applicant fails to demonstrate the applicant's ability to maintain adequate premises liability and casualty insurance for its proposed marihuana facility.

(f) The applicant holds an elective office of a governmental unit of this state, another state, or the federal government; is a member of or employed by a regulatory body of a governmental unit in this state, another state, or the federal government; or is employed by a governmental unit of this state. This subdivision does not apply to an elected officer of or employee of a federally recognized Indian tribe or to an elected precinct delegate.

(g) The applicant, if an individual, has been a resident of this state for less than a continuous 2-year period immediately preceding the date of filing the application. The requirements in this subdivision do not apply after June 30, 2018.

(h) The board determines that the applicant is not in compliance with section 205(1).

(i) The applicant fails to meet other criteria established by rule.

(3) In determining whether to grant a license to an applicant, the board may also consider all of the following:

(a) The integrity, moral character, and reputation; personal and business probity; financial ability and experience; and responsibility or means to operate or maintain a marihuana facility of the applicant and of any other person that meets either of the following:

(i) Controls, directly or indirectly, the applicant.

(ii) Is controlled, directly or indirectly, by the applicant or by a person who controls, directly or indirectly, the applicant.

(b) The financial ability of the applicant to purchase and maintain adequate liability and casualty insurance.

(c) The sources and total amount of the applicant's capitalization to operate and maintain the proposed marihuana facility.

(d) Whether the applicant has been indicted for, charged with, arrested for, or convicted of, pled guilty or nolo contendere to, forfeited bail concerning, or had expunged any relevant criminal offense under the laws of any jurisdiction, either felony or misdemeanor, not including traffic violations, regardless of whether the offense has been expunged, pardoned, or reversed on appeal or otherwise.

(e) Whether the applicant has filed, or had filed against it, a proceeding for bankruptcy within the past 7 years.

(f) Whether the applicant has been served with a complaint or other notice filed with any public body regarding payment of any tax required under federal, state, or local law that has been delinquent for 1 or more years.

(g) Whether the applicant has a history of noncompliance with any regulatory requirements in this state or any other jurisdiction.

(h) Whether at the time of application the applicant is a defendant in litigation involving its business practices.

(i) Whether the applicant meets other standards in rules applicable to the license category.

(4) Each applicant shall submit with its application, on forms provided by the board, a passport quality photograph and shall ensure that 1 set of fingerprints is submitted to the department of state police for each person having any ownership interest in the marihuana facility and each person who is an officer, director, or managerial employee of the applicant, in order for the department of state police to conduct a criminal history check on each person and to forward each person's fingerprints to the Federal Bureau of Investigation for a national criminal history check. The applicant shall submit with its application each person's written consent to the criminal history check described in this section and the submission of each person's fingerprints to, and the inclusion of each person's fingerprints in, the state and federal database systems described in subsection (7).

(5) The fingerprints required under subsection (4) may be taken by a law enforcement agency or any other person determined by the department of state police to be qualified to take fingerprints. The applicant shall submit a fingerprint processing fee to the department in an amount required under section 3 of 1935 PA 120, MCL 28.273, and any costs imposed by the Federal Bureau of Investigation.

(6) The department of state police shall conduct a criminal history check on each person described in subsection (4) and shall request the Federal Bureau of Investigation to make a determination of the existence of any national criminal history pertaining to each person. The department of state police shall provide the board with a written report containing the criminal history record information

of each person who was the subject of the criminal history check conducted under this section.

(7) All of the following apply concerning fingerprints submitted to the department of state police under this section:

(a) The department of state police shall store and retain all fingerprints submitted under this section in an automated fingerprint identification system database that searches against latent fingerprints, and provides for an automatic notification if and when a subsequent fingerprint is submitted into the system that matches a set of fingerprints previously submitted under this section or if and when the criminal history of an individual whose fingerprints are retained in the system is updated. Upon receiving a notification, the department of state police shall immediately notify the board. Information in the database maintained under this subsection is confidential, is not subject to disclosure under the freedom of information act, 1976 PA 442, MCL 15.231 to 15.246, and shall not be disclosed to any person except for purposes of this act or for law enforcement purposes.

(b) The department of state police shall forward all fingerprints submitted to it under this section to the Federal Bureau of Investigation for submission of those fingerprints into the FBI automatic notification system. This subdivision does not apply until the department of state police is a participant in the FBI automatic notification system. As used in this subdivision:

(i) "Automatic notification system" means a system that stores and retains fingerprints, and that provides for an automatic notification to a participant if and when a fingerprint is submitted into the system that matches an individual whose fingerprints are retained in the system or if and when the criminal history of an individual whose fingerprints are retained in the system is updated.

(ii) "FBI automatic notification system" means the automatic notification system that is maintained by the Federal Bureau of Investigation.

(8) The board shall review all applications for licenses and shall inform each applicant of the board's decision.

(9) A license shall be issued for a 1-year period and is renewable annually. Except as otherwise provided in this act, the board shall renew a license if all of the following requirements are met:

(a) The licensee applies to the board on a renewal form provided by the board that requires information prescribed in rules.

(b) The application is received by the board on or before the expiration date of the current license.

(c) The licensee pays the regulatory assessment under section 603.

(d) The licensee meets the requirements of this act and any other renewal requirements set forth in rules.

(10) The department shall notify the licensee by mail or electronic mail at the last known address on file with the board advising of the time, procedure, and regulatory assessment under section 603. The failure of the licensee to receive notice under this subsection does not relieve the licensee of the responsibility for renewing the license.

(11) If a license renewal application is not submitted by the license expiration date, the license may be renewed within 60 days after its expiration date upon application, payment of the regulatory assessment under section 603, and satisfaction of any renewal requirement and late fee set forth in rules. The licensee may continue to operate during the 60 days after the license expiration date if the license is renewed by the end of the 60-day period.

(12) License expiration does not terminate the board's authority to impose sanctions on a licensee whose license has expired.

(13) In its decision on an application for renewal, the board shall consider any specific written input it receives from an individual or entity within the local unit of government in which the applicant for renewal is located.

(14) A licensee must consent in writing to inspections, examinations, searches, and seizures that are permitted under this act and must provide a handwriting exemplar, fingerprints, photographs, and information as authorized in this act or by rules.

(15) An applicant or licensee has a continuing duty to provide information requested by the board and to cooperate in any investigation, inquiry, or hearing conducted by the board.

MCL § 333.27404 True party of interest.

(1) The board shall issue a license only in the name of the true party of interest.

(2) For the following true parties of interest, information concerning the indicated individuals must be included in the disclosures required of an applicant or licensee:

> (a) For an individual or sole proprietorship: the proprietor and spouse.
>
> (b) For a partnership and limited liability partnership: all partners and their spouses. For a limited partnership and limited liability limited partnership: all general and limited partners and their spouses. For a limited liability company: all members, managers, and their spouses.

(c) For a privately held corporation: all corporate officers or persons with equivalent titles and their spouses and all stockholders and their spouses.

(d) For a publicly held corporation: all corporate officers or persons with equivalent titles and their spouses.

(e) For a multilevel ownership enterprise: any entity or person that receives or has the right to receive a percentage of the gross or net profit from the enterprise during any full or partial calendar or fiscal year.

(f) For a nonprofit corporation: all individuals and entities with membership or shareholder rights in accordance with the articles of incorporation or the bylaws and their spouses.

(3) For purposes of this section, "true party of interest" does not mean:

(a) A person or entity receiving reasonable payment for rent on a fixed basis under a bona fide lease or rental obligation, unless the lessor or property manager exercises control over or participates in the management of the business.

(b) A person who receives a bonus as an employee if the employee is on a fixed wage or salary and the bonus is not more than 25% of the employee's prebonus annual compensation or if the bonus is based on a written incentive/bonus program that is not out of the ordinary for the services rendered.

MCL § 333.27405 Background check.

Subject to the laws of this state, before hiring a prospective employee, the holder of a license shall conduct a background check of the prospective employee. If the background check indicates a pending charge or conviction within the past 10 years for a controlled substance-related felony, a licensee shall not hire the prospective employee without written permission of the board.

MCL § 333.27406 Transfer, sale, or purchase of license.

Each license is exclusive to the licensee, and a licensee or any other person must apply for and receive the board's approval before a license is transferred, sold, or purchased. The attempted transfer, sale, or other conveyance of an interest of more than 1% in a license without prior board approval is grounds for suspension or revocation of the license or for other sanction considered appropriate by the board.

MCL § 333.27407 Denial, suspension, revocation, or restriction of license.

(1) If an applicant or licensee fails to comply with this act or rules, if a licensee fails to comply with the marihuana tracking act, if a licensee no longer meets the eligibility requirements for a license under this act, or if an applicant or licensee fails to provide information the board requests to assist in any investigation, inquiry, or board hearing, the board may deny, suspend, revoke, or restrict a license. The board may suspend, revoke, or restrict a license and require the removal of a licensee or an employee of a licensee for a violation of this act, rules, the marihuana tracking act, or any ordinance adopted under section 205. The board may impose civil fines of up to $5,000.00 against an individual and up to $10,000.00 or an amount equal to the daily gross receipts, whichever is greater, against a licensee for each violation of this act, rules, or an order of the board. Assessment of a civil fine under this subsection is not a bar to the investigation, arrest, charging, or prosecution of an individual for any other violation of this act and is not grounds to suppress evidence in any criminal prosecution that arises under this act or any other law of this state.

(2) The board shall comply with the administrative procedures act of 1969, 1969 PA 306, MCL 24.201 to 24.328, when denying,

revoking, suspending, or restricting a license or imposing a fine. The board may suspend a license without notice or hearing upon a determination that the safety or health of patrons or employees is jeopardized by continuing a marihuana facility's operation. If the board suspends a license under this subsection without notice or hearing, a prompt postsuspension hearing must be held to determine if the suspension should remain in effect. The suspension may remain in effect until the board determines that the cause for suspension has been abated. The board may revoke the license or approve a transfer or sale of the license upon a determination that the licensee has not made satisfactory progress toward abating the hazard.

(3) After denying an application for a license, the board shall, upon request, provide a public investigative hearing at which the applicant is given the opportunity to present testimony and evidence to establish its suitability for a license. Other testimony and evidence may be presented at the hearing, but the board's decision must be based on the whole record before the board and is not limited to testimony and evidence submitted at the public investigative hearing.

(4) Except for license applicants who may be granted a hearing at the discretion of the board under subsection (3), any party aggrieved by an action of the board suspending, revoking, restricting, or refusing to renew a license, or imposing a fine, shall be given a hearing before the board upon request. A request for a hearing must be made to the board in writing within 21 days after service of notice of the action of the board. Notice of the action of the board must be served either by personal delivery or by certified mail, postage prepaid, to the aggrieved party. Notice served by certified mail is considered complete on the business day following the date of the mailing.

(5) The board may conduct investigative and contested case hearings; issue subpoenas for the attendance of witnesses; issue subpoenas duces tecum for the production of books, ledgers, records,

memoranda, electronically retrievable data, and other pertinent documents; and administer oaths and affirmations to witnesses as appropriate to exercise and discharge the powers and duties of the board under this act. The executive director or his or her designee may issue subpoenas and administer oaths and affirmations to witnesses.

MCL § 333.27501 Grower license.

(1) A grower license authorizes the grower to grow not more than the following number of marihuana plants under the indicated license class for each license the grower holds in that class:

(a) Class A – 500 marihuana plants.

(b) Class B – 1,000 marihuana plants.

(c) Class C – 1,500 marihuana plants.

(2) A grower license authorizes sale of marihuana seeds or marihuana plants only to a grower by means of a secure transporter.

(3) A grower license authorizes sale of marihuana, other than seeds, only to a processor or provisioning center.

(4) A grower license authorizes the grower to transfer marihuana only by means of a secure transporter.

(5) To be eligible for a grower license, the applicant and each investor in the grower must not have an interest in a secure transporter or safety compliance facility.

(6) A grower shall comply with all of the following:

(a) Until December 31, 2021, have, or have as an active employee an individual who has, a minimum of 2 years' experience as a registered primary caregiver.

(b) While holding a license as a grower, not be a registered primary caregiver and not employ an individual who is simultaneously a registered primary caregiver.

(c) Enter all transactions, current inventory, and other information into the statewide monitoring system as required in this act, rules, and the marihuana tracking act.

(7) A grower license does not authorize the grower to operate in an area unless the area is zoned for industrial or agricultural uses or is unzoned and otherwise meets the requirements established in section 205(1).

MCL § 333.27502 Processor license.

(1) A processor license authorizes purchase of marihuana only from a grower and sale of marihuana-infused products or marihuana only to a provisioning center.

(2) A processor license authorizes the processor to transfer marihuana only by means of a secure transporter.

(3) To be eligible for a processor license, the applicant and each investor in the processor must not have an interest in a secure transporter or safety compliance facility.

(4) A processor shall comply with all of the following:

(a) Until December 31, 2021, have, or have as an active employee an individual who has, a minimum of 2 years' experience as a registered primary caregiver.

(b) While holding a license as a processor, not be a registered primary caregiver and not employ an individual who is simultaneously a registered primary caregiver.

(c) Enter all transactions, current inventory, and other information into the statewide monitoring system as required in this act, rules, and the marihuana tracking act.

MCL § 333.27503 Secure transporter license.

(1) A secure transporter license authorizes the licensee to store and transport marihuana and money associated with the purchase or sale of marihuana between marihuana facilities for a fee upon request of a person with legal custody of that marihuana or money. It does not authorize transport to a registered qualifying patient or registered primary caregiver.

(2) To be eligible for a secure transporter license, the applicant and each investor with an interest in the secure transporter must not have an interest in a grower, processor, provisioning center, or safety compliance facility and must not be a registered qualifying patient or a registered primary caregiver.

(3) A secure transporter shall enter all transactions, current inventory, and other information into the statewide monitoring system as required in this act, rules, and the marihuana tracking act.

(4) A secure transporter shall comply with all of the following:

(a) Each driver transporting marihuana must have a chauffeur's license issued by this state.

(b) Each employee who has custody of marihuana or money that is related to a marihuana transaction shall not have been convicted of or released from incarceration for a felony under the laws of this state, any other state, or the United States within the past 5 years or have been convicted of a misdemeanor involving a controlled substance within the past 5 years.

(c) Each vehicle shall be operated with a 2-person crew with at least 1 individual remaining with the vehicle at all times during the transportation of marihuana.

(d) A route plan and manifest shall be entered into the statewide monitoring system, and a copy shall be carried in the transporting vehicle and presented to a law enforcement officer upon request.

(e) The marihuana shall be transported in 1 or more sealed containers and not be accessible while in transit.

(f) A secure transporting vehicle shall not bear markings or other indication that it is carrying marihuana or a marihuana-infused product.

(5) A secure transporter is subject to administrative inspection by a law enforcement officer at any point during the transportation of marihuana to determine compliance with this act.

MCL § 333.27504 Provisioning center license.

(1) A provisioning center license authorizes the purchase or transfer of marihuana only from a grower or processor and sale or transfer to only a registered qualifying patient or registered primary caregiver. All transfers of marihuana to a provisioning center from a separate marihuana facility shall be by means of a secure transporter.

(2) A provisioning center license authorizes the provisioning center to transfer marihuana to or from a safety compliance facility for testing by means of a secure transporter.

(3) To be eligible for a provisioning center license, the applicant and each investor in the provisioning center must not have an interest in a secure transporter or safety compliance facility.

(4) A provisioning center shall comply with all of the following:

(a) Sell or transfer marihuana to a registered qualifying patient or registered primary caregiver only after it has been tested and bears the label required for retail sale.

(b) Enter all transactions, current inventory, and other information into the statewide monitoring system as required in this act, rules, and the marihuana tracking act.

(c) Before selling or transferring marihuana to a registered qualifying patient or to a registered primary caregiver on behalf of a registered qualifying patient, inquire of the statewide monitoring system to determine whether the patient and, if applicable, the caregiver hold a valid, current, unexpired, and unrevoked registry identification card and that the sale or transfer will not exceed the daily purchasing limit established by the medical marihuana licensing board under this act.

(d) Not allow the sale, consumption, or use of alcohol or tobacco products on the premises.

(e) Not allow a physician to conduct a medical examination or issue a medical certification document on the premises for the purpose of obtaining a registry identification card.

MCL § 333.27505 Safety compliance facility license.

(1) In addition to transfer and testing authorized in section 203, a safety compliance facility license authorizes the facility to receive marihuana from, test marihuana for, and return marihuana to only a marihuana facility.

(2) A safety compliance facility must be accredited by an entity approved by the board by 1 year after the date the license is issued

or have previously provided drug testing services to this state or this state's court system and be a vendor in good standing in regard to those services. The board may grant a variance from this requirement upon a finding that the variance is necessary to protect and preserve the public health, safety, or welfare.

(3) To be eligible for a safety compliance facility license, the applicant and each investor with any interest in the safety compliance facility must not have an interest in a grower, secure transporter, processor, or provisioning center.

(4) A safety compliance facility shall comply with all of the following:

(a) Perform tests to certify that marihuana is reasonably free of chemical residues such as fungicides and insecticides.

(b) Use validated test methods to determine tetrahydrocannabinol, tetrahydrocannabinol acid, cannabidiol, and cannabidiol acid levels.

(c) Perform tests that determine whether marihuana complies with the standards the board establishes for microbial and mycotoxin contents.

(d) Perform other tests necessary to determine compliance with any other good manufacturing practices as prescribed in rules.

(e) Enter all transactions, current inventory, and other information into the statewide monitoring system as required in this act, rules, and the marihuana tracking act.

(f) Have a secured laboratory space that cannot be accessed by the general public.

(g) Retain and employ at least 1 staff member with a relevant advanced degree in a medical or laboratory science.

MCL § 333.27801 Marihuana advisory panel.

(1) The marihuana advisory panel is created within the department.

(2) The marihuana advisory panel shall consist of 17 members, including the director of state police or his or her designee, the director of this state's department of health and human services or his or her designee, the director of the department of licensing and regulatory affairs or his or her designee, the attorney general or his or her designee, the director of the department of agriculture and rural development or his or her designee, and the following members appointed by the governor:

(a) One registered medical marihuana patient or medical marihuana primary caregiver.

(b) One representative of growers.

(c) One representative of processors.

(d) One representative of provisioning centers.

(e) One representative of safety compliance facilities.

(f) One representative of townships.

(g) One representative of cities and villages.

(h) One representative of counties.

(i) One representative of sheriffs.

(j) One representative of local police.

(k) One physician licensed under article 15 of the public health code, 1978 PA 368, MCL 333.16101 to 333.18838.

(l) One representative of a secure transporter.

(3) The members first appointed to the panel shall be appointed within 3 months after the effective date of this act and shall serve at the pleasure of the governor. Appointed members of the panel shall serve for terms of 3 years or until a successor is appointed, whichever is later.

(4) If a vacancy occurs on the advisory panel, the governor shall make an appointment for the unexpired term in the same manner as the original appointment.

(5) The first meeting of the panel shall be called by the director of the department or his or her designee within 1 month after the advisory panel is appointed. At the first meeting, the panel shall elect from among its members a chairperson and any other officers it considers necessary or appropriate. After the first meeting, the panel shall meet at least 2 times each year, or more frequently at the call of the chairperson.

(6) A majority of the members of the panel constitute a quorum for the transaction of business. A majority of the members present and serving are required for official action of the panel.

(7) The business that the panel performs shall be conducted at a public meeting held in compliance with the open meetings act, 1976 PA 267, MCL 15.261 to 15.275.

(8) A writing prepared, owned, used, in the possession of, or retained by the panel in the performance of an official function is subject to the freedom of information act, 1976 PA 442, MCL 15.231 to 15.246.

(9) Members of the panel shall serve without compensation. However, members of the panel may be reimbursed for their actual and necessary expenses incurred in the performance of their official duties as members of the panel.

(10) The panel may make recommendations to the board concerning promulgation of rules and, as requested by the board or the department, the administration, implementation, and enforcement of this act and the marihuana tracking act.

(11) State departments and agencies shall cooperate with the panel and, upon request, provide it with meeting space and other necessary resources to assist it in the performance of its duties.

APPENDIX C

MARIHUANA TRACKING ACT

Act 282 of 2016 (EXCERPT)

MCL § 333.27901 Short title.

This act shall be known and may be cited as the "marihuana tracking act".

MCL § 333.27902 Definitions.

As used in this act:

(a) "Department" means the department of licensing and regulatory affairs.

(b) "Licensee" means that term as defined in section 102 of the medical marihuana facilities licensing act.

(c) "Marihuana" means that term as defined in section 7106 of the public health code, 1978 PA 368, MCL 333.7106.

(d) "Registered primary caregiver" means that term as defined in section 102 of the medical marihuana facilities licensing act.

(e) "Registered qualifying patient" means that term as defined in section 102 of the medical marihuana facilities licensing act.

(f) "Registry identification card" means that term as defined in section 3 of the Michigan medical marihuana act, 2008 IL 1, MCL 333.26423.

(g) "Statewide monitoring system" or "system" means an internet-based, statewide database established, implemented, and maintained directly or indirectly by the department that is available to licensees, law enforcement agencies, and authorized state departments and agencies on a 24-hour basis for all of the following:

(i) Verifying registry identification cards.

(ii) Tracking marihuana transfer and transportation by licensees, including transferee, date, quantity, and price.

(iii) Verifying in a commercially reasonable time that a transfer will not exceed the limit that the registered qualifying patient or registered primary caregiver is authorized to receive under section 4 of the Michigan medical marihuana act, 2008 IL 1, MCL 333.26424.

MCL § 333.27903 Statewide monitoring system; use as integrated marihuana tracking, inventory, and verification system; requirements; rules; bids; violation; termination of contract.

(1) The department shall establish a statewide monitoring system for use as an integrated marihuana tracking, inventory, and verification system. The system must allow for interface with third-party inventory and tracking systems as described in section 207 of the medical marihuana facilities licensing act to provide for access by this state, licensees, and law enforcement personnel, to the extent that they need and are authorized to receive or submit the information, to comply with, enforce, or administer this act; the Michigan

medical marihuana act, 2008 IL 1, MCL 333.26421 to 333.26430; or the medical marihuana facilities licensing act.

(2) At a minimum, the system must be capable of storing and providing access to information that, in conjunction with 1 or more third-party inventory control and tracking systems under section 207 of the medical marihuana facilities licensing act, allows all of the following:

(a) Verification that a registry identification card is current and valid and has not been suspended, revoked, or denied.

(b) Retention of a record of the date, time, quantity, and price of each sale or transfer of marihuana to a registered qualifying patient or registered primary caregiver.

(c) Determination of whether a particular sale or transfer transaction will exceed the permissible limit established under the Michigan medical marihuana act, 2008 IL 1, MCL 333.26421 to 333.26430.

(d) Effective monitoring of marihuana seed-to-sale transfers.

(e) Receipt and integration of information from third-party inventory control and tracking systems under section 207 of the medical marihuana facilities licensing act.

(3) The department shall promulgate rules to govern the process for incorporating information concerning registry identification card renewal, revocation, suspension, and changes and other information applicable to licensees, registered primary caregivers, and registered qualifying patients that must be included and maintained in the statewide monitoring system.

(4) The department shall seek bids to establish, operate, and maintain the statewide monitoring system under this section. The department shall do all of the following:

(a) Evaluate bidders based on the cost of the service and the ability to meet all of the requirements of this act; the Michigan medical marihuana act, 2008 IL 1, MCL 333.26421 to 333.26430; and the medical marihuana facilities licensing act.

(b) Give strong consideration to the bidder's ability to prevent fraud, abuse, and other unlawful or prohibited activities associated with the commercial trade in marihuana in this state, and the ability to provide additional tools for the administration and enforcement of this act; the Michigan medical marihuana act, 2008 IL 1, MCL 333.26421 to 333.26430; and the medical marihuana facilities licensing act.

(c) Institute procedures to ensure that the contract awardee does not disclose or use the information in the system for any use or purpose except for the enforcement, oversight, and implementation of the Michigan medical marihuana act, 2008 IL 1, MCL 333.26421 to 333.26430, or the medical marihuana facilities licensing act.

(d) Require the contract awardee to deliver the functioning system by 180 days after award of the contract.

(5) The department may terminate a contract with a contract awardee under this act for a violation of this act. A contract awardee may be debarred from award of other state contracts under this act for a violation of this act.

MCL § 333.27904 Confidentiality; exemption from disclosure.

The information in the system is confidential and is exempt from disclosure under the freedom of information act, 1976 PA 442, MCL 15.231 to 15.246. Information in the system may be disclosed for purposes of enforcing this act; the Michigan medical marihuana act, 2008 IL 1, MCL 333.26421 to 333.26430; and the medical marihuana facilities licensing act.

www.ingramcontent.com/pod-product-compliance
Lightning Source LLC
LaVergne TN
LVHW052314200926
848481LV00002B/556
* 9 7 8 0 6 9 2 9 6 8 3 4 5 *